Categories We Live By

*The Construction of Sex, Gender,
Race, and Other Social Categories*

ÁSTA

OXFORD
UNIVERSITY PRESS

OXFORD
UNIVERSITY PRESS

Oxford University Press is a department of the University of Oxford. It furthers
the University's objective of excellence in research, scholarship, and education
by publishing worldwide. Oxford is a registered trade mark of Oxford University
Press in the UK and certain other countries.

Published in the United States of America by Oxford University Press
198 Madison Avenue, New York, NY 10016, United States of America.

Library of Congress Cataloging-in-Publication Data
Names: Ásta, author.
Title: Categories we live by : the construction of sex, gender, race, and other
social categories / Ásta.
Description: New York, NY, United States of America : Oxford University Press, [2018] |
Includes bibliographical references and index.
Identifiers: LCCN 2017059872 (print) | LCCN 2018020333 (ebook) | ISBN 9780190256821
(online course) | ISBN 9780190256814 (updf) | ISBN 9780190256807 (pbk. : alk. paper) |
ISBN 9780190256791 (cloth : alk. paper)
Subjects: LCSH: Group identity. | Population.
Classification: LCC HM753 (ebook) | LCC HM753.S94 2018 (print) | DDC 305—dc23
LC record available at https://lccn.loc.gov/2017059872

Categories We Live By

Studies in Feminist Philosophy is designed to showcase cutting-edge monographs and collections that display the full range of feminist approaches to philosophy, that push feminist thought in important new directions, and that display the outstanding quality of feminist philosophical thought.

STUDIES IN FEMINIST PHILOSOPHY

Published in the Series:

Handa Dore, Þóru yngri, Þóru eldri, Sveini, og Sally

CONTENTS

ACKNOWLEDGMENTS

I am indebted to many people for feedback, support, and conversations related to material in this book. I would like to thank Linda Alcoff, Elizabeth Barnes, Erin Beeghly, Aaron Bentley, Talia Bettcher, the late Kalman Bland, Garrett Bredeson, Sylvain Bromberger, Åsa Burman, Alex Byrne, Cheshire Calhoun, Rachel Cooper, Ann Cudd, Robin Dembroff, Esa Díaz-León, Andy Egan, Jeanna Eichenbaum, the late Iris Einheuser, Brian Epstein, Matthew Eshleman, Eyja Margrét Brynjarsdóttir, Barbara Fultner, Ann Garry, Nathaniel Goldberg, Rebecca Groves, Carol Gould, Kim Q. Hall, Kristin Hanson, Haraldur Ólafsson, Elizabeth Harman, Dana Harvey, Kattis Honkanen, Jennifer Hudin, Andrew Janiak, Ada Jaarsma, Marija Jankovic, Katharine Jenkins, Stephanie Kapusta, Abigail Klassen, Beatrice Kobow, Colin Koopman, Rae Langton, Francesca Lattanzi, Hilde Lindemann, Jamie Lindsay, Kirk Ludwig, Rebecca Mason, Mary Kate McGowen, Sarah McGrath, Fiona Macpherson, Katalin Makkai, Ishani Maitra, Ron Mallon, Kate Marshall, Jennifer McKitrick, Mari Mikkola, Uma Narayan, Ian Newman, Olga Bergmann, Jeffrey Paris, Caroline Perry, Elizabeth Potter, Lucy Randall, Agustín Rayo, Katherine Ritchie, Joshua Rivkin, Adina Roskies, Abraham Roth, Dennis Rothermel, Jocelyn Saidenberg, Cat Saint-Croix, David Sanford, Marya Schechtman, Michael Schmitz, John Searle, Paul Sherwin, Laurie Shrage, Anita Silvers, Walter Sinnott-Armstrong, Sigríður Þorgeirsdóttir, Rebecca Solnit, Alice Sowaal, Natalie Stoljar, Abraham Stone, Robert Stalnaker, Christopher Sturr, Sveinn Einarsson, Jacqueline Taylor, Brian Thomas, Amie Thomasson, Bas van Fraassen, Marga Vega, Blakey Vermeule, Catherine Wearing, Ralph Wedgwood,

Annabel Wharton, Tiffany Willoughby-Herard, Rasmus Grønfeldt Winther, Stephen Yablo, Þóra Kristjánsdóttir, and Þórður Harðarson.

I owe a special debt to Louise Antony, Jennifer Church, Catherine Z. Elgin, Anna Hallin, Sally Haslanger, Helen Longino, Rebecca McLennan, Dore Bowen Solomon, Judith Jarvis Thomson, Shelley Wilcox, and Charlotte Witt.

None of the people I have mentioned are responsible for the views expressed herein or any remaining errors. The same holds for authors cited or mentioned in the text.

I am grateful for the support I have had for my work at San Francisco State University and of the Ruth W. and A. Morris Williams, Jr. Fellowship at The National Humanities Center 2016–2017, which allowed me to complete the manuscript.

PERMISSIONS

I am grateful for the permission to use material from previously published papers:

Chapter One draws on material in "Essentiality Conferred", *Philosophical Studies*, July 2008. Springer.

Chapter Two draws on material in "The Social Construction of Human Kinds", *Hypatia*, Fall 2013, vol. 28(4) (Wiley); "Social Construction", *Philosophy Compass* (Wiley, December 2015); and "Social Kinds", *The Routledge Handbook on Collective Intentionality*, ed. by Kirk Ludwig and Marija Jankovic (Routledge 2017).

Chapter Three is based in large part on "The Metaphysics of Sex and Gender". *Feminist Metaphysics*, ed. by Charlotte Witt (Springer, 2011).

Chapter Four draws on material in "The Social Construction of Human Kinds", *Hypatia*, Fall 2013, vol. 28(4) (Wiley), "The Metaphysics of Sex and Gender", *Feminist Metaphysics*, ed. by Charlotte Witt (Springer, 2011), and reviews of *The Metaphysics of Gender*, by Charlotte Witt in *Notre Dame Philosophical Reviews*, May 2012 and *The Philosophers' Magazine*, Second Quarter, 2012.

Cover art: Cluster from the *Conspiracy of Pleasure* series and is copyrighted by Anna Hallin. http://this.is/ahallin/

Categories We Live By

Introduction
Social Categories

IN *INFINITE CITY: A SAN FRANCISCO ATLAS* (Solnit 2010), Rebecca Solnit and Guillermo Gómez-Peña reflect on their experience as they travel through the city of San Francisco. Solnit experiences herself as Western in Chinatown, as white in Bayview, as straight and female in the Castro. Gómez-Peña is mistaken for a tourist from Argentina in Chinatown, at the Bollywood Café he is "the wrong kind of brown", in the Castro he is an older gay man, and in the financial district he is nobody.

All of these—Western, white, and so on—are examples of properties that define social categories, and although they vary in importance and pervasiveness, these categories set parameters for the encounters Solnit and Gómez-Peña have with people on their wanderings through the city.

While it is often only when we travel out of our comfort zones that we become aware of the many social categories we belong to, they are also there when we are comfortably not aware of them, framing our interactions with other people and our own self-understanding. But what are social categories? How are they created and sustained? How do they shape our interactions and our self-understanding? This book is dedicated to these questions.

Answering these questions amounts to giving a metaphysics of social categories—a theory of the nature of social categories. My strategy will be to give a metaphysics of the properties or features that define them. For example, if the category is *women*, then the property is *being a woman*; if the category is *queers*, then the property is *being queer*, and so on.[1]

---

[1] It is important that we talk of "being queer" as opposed to "queerness", since the latter is a reified property and thus a logical object. Also, a note on terminology: a "category", in my usage, refers to

What makes a category of humans social? How can we tell whether a particular category is social as opposed to, say, natural? I offer answers to such questions in these pages. The brief answer is simple: if it is defined by a social property or feature, it is a social category; if by a natural feature, a natural one. But this simple answer may be of little help if we don't know what a social property is and how to detect one, as we won't be able to tell whether a particular property is social or otherwise.

The longer answer to the question starts with the intuition that we have social properties in virtue of something about other people. Carving out an account of social properties will involve finding a clear articulation of that intuition.

My methodological approach is to have in sight paradigm cases of social properties and of properties that are not social and then to offer an account that gets the paradigm cases right. I take it that being a president and being popular are paradigm cases of social properties and having red hair is a paradigm case of a property that isn't social. I offer a framework, which I call a "conferralist" framework, that makes sense of these paradigm cases of social property. I then later argue that some properties, which there is dispute about, are also social, because they have the same structure as the paradigm social cases and because of their role in explanation. The many disputed cases include the categories that offered special protections in various jurisdictions because of the historical and current mistreatment of its members in the culture, such as gender, sex, race, religion, disability, and sexual orientation categories, but also many others.

In the first chapter, I introduce the *conferralist* framework that plays multiple roles in this book. On my view, a social property of an individual is one that one has because of something about other people, and the conferralist framework captures that intuition: it is a property that someone has conferred on them by others. This property is a social status consisting in constraints on and enablements to the individual's behavior in a context (behavioral constraints and enablements). How does this property get conferred? The answer to that depends on which property we are talking about, and the conferralist framework is an abstract schema that needs to be filled in for each property. However, the central cases of conferred properties that concern this project all share that there is another property, which I call a "base" property, that the conferrers are attempting to track

---

a class of objects or stuffs defined by the unifying property. It is thus in the world, so to speak, as opposed to a mental or semantic entity. I use "category" and "kind" interchangeably in this book.

in their conferral.[2] The individuals in question may or may not have this base property, but what is important is that they are taken to have it and get conferred on them a social status on that basis. Herein lies an analysis of what it is for a feature of an individual to have social significance in a context: *a feature is socially significant in a context in which people taken to have the feature get conferred onto them a social status*. Giving an account of social categories thus comes down to giving an account of what it is for a feature of an individual to have social significance. In giving such an account, a new conception of social construction emerges. I call this conception "social construction as social significance" and place it in the context of other conceptions of social construction in chapter 2, "Social Construction as Social Significance."

There has been much discussion in various disciplines in the last thirty years about social construction, and there are a lot of different things that people want to capture with that notion. The phenomenon I want to capture is when some feature of an individual takes on *social significance*, for instance, when exhibiting certain secondary sex characteristics constrains what roles a person can play at home and in civic and professional life; or when exhibiting certain morphological features associated with geographical ancestry does so.

After offering a general conception of social construction, I turn to the project of offering specific accounts of the various social categories that shape our lives and their particular construction. Readers may or may not like my particular proposals, but that in itself does not speak against the general framework I'm offering, and readers may use the general framework to offer different specific proposals of their own of the various social categories.

To set up my own accounts of gender and sex, I offer in chapter 3 an interpretation of the dominant accounts of sex and gender in feminist theory of the last few decades, the post-Beauvoirean one and Judith Butler's.

I then turn to my own conferralist accounts of sex, gender, and LGBTQ status in chapter 4 and some other dominant social categories such as race, religion, and disability in chapter 5. I compare the conferralist account of these categories to some prominent views of those categories in the literature.

---

[2] There can be exceptions to this, where there is no base property, but such cases are not central to the present analysis of social categories. I address a counterexample to that claim in chapter 2. Note also that sometime it is the base property itself that is the focus in the conferral, and sometimes it is another feature that is taken as evidence of the presence of the base property.

The conferralist framework can be used to make sense of any social category. I show it in action by offering accounts of some of the most dominant social categories, but it can be used to account for any others. The categories that are legally protected in various jurisdictions[3] are of special importance to my analysis, however, as I maintain there is a need for legal protection in these cases precisely because features of members of these groups are socially significant in the way my analysis explains.

I started by asking what social categories are and how they are constructed and maintained. The theoretical machinery I have mentioned is brought in to answer those questions. But I also maintained that social categories shape our interactions and our self-understanding. In order to make good on those claims, I offer an account of identity that fits with the account of social categories offered. I turn to that task in chapter 6, "Identity as Social Location." Introducing an account of identity allows me to offer a fuller picture of the dynamic construction of social categories and of our role in that construction.

My motivation for giving a metaphysics of social categories is fueled by the awareness that, while social categories can be a positive source of identity and belonging, they often are oppressive, and membership in them can put serious constraints on a person's life options. So, in offering my theory of social categories, the aim is to reveal the cogs and belts and arrangements of parts in machines that often are oppressive. Doing so also serves to support work done in the humanities and social sciences on the role of social construction in generating and upholding oppressive practices and institutions. While it has become commonplace in many academic disciplines to say that various categories are socially constructed, a defensible theory of social construction that can support those claims has been lacking. There is an increased interest among philosophers in engaging with such positions, but so far, attempts at such an engagement have done little to alleviate a widespread skepticism in philosophical circles, where it is commonly held that the claim that something is socially constructed, understood as a metaphysical thesis, is at best false, at worst incoherent. I hope that the framework I offer can support social constructionist claims about the various categories we find ourselves in and that I thereby give the skeptics a defensible theory to engage with.

This book project lies at the intersection of social metaphysics, social philosophy, and feminist philosophy. While it is a work in feminist

---

[3] Such as sex, gender, race, disability, sexual orientation, gender identity, religion, etc.

analytic metaphysics, a central component of the account is a plausible account of the interplay of categorization, agency, and identity, and, in that, the views presented draw on work in both the analytic and the continental tradition. This is especially prominent in the last component of the book, where I give the fuller picture of the mechanics of social categories and attend to the fact that the behavioral constraints and enablements are the product of our membership in many intersecting social categories. This fuller picture takes account of individual agents' roles in their placement in social categories and the aforementioned intersectional complexities by unpacking the metaphor of *social identity as social location*.

Given that the motivation for the project is to offer an analysis of social categories that can aid in fighting oppression, it is imperative that my account be able to explain the systematic nature of oppression. In the last chapter, I address briefly how an account of social categories that has them constructed and maintained by the actions of individual agents in contexts can nevertheless explain the systematic features of categories that can both be what grounds solidarity and be the starting point for political action.

I say that this is a work of feminist analytic metaphysics. Let me elaborate on what I take that to mean.

To do philosophy as a feminist involves certain commitments. Allowing myself the broad strokes, I see feminist activism as being about ending the oppression of women and feminist theorizing as being about developing theoretical tools that can help that activism, both by deepening our understanding of phenomena and by leading us in our search for change.

This book is a work of feminist theorizing in which I develop theoretical tools to help us understand social categories and the mechanisms by which we inhabit them. It is not an attempt to theorize about people's experiences directly, but rather an aspect of their social environment that influences that experience. Although the theorizing is in that sense abstract, given that its aim is a deeper understanding of various social mechanics that contribute to injustice, the theorizing itself needs to be done with appropriate care. María Lugones and Elizabeth Spelman (1983) called attention to that issue in an article they published together many moons ago:

> What are the things we need to know about others, and about ourselves, in order to speak intelligently, intelligibly, sensitively, and helpfully about their lives? We can show respect, or lack of it, in writing theoretically about others no less than in talking directly with them. This is not to say that here we have a well-worked out concept of respect, but only to suggest that together all of us consider what it would mean to theorize in a respectful way.

When we speak, write, and publish our theories, to whom do we think we are accountable? (579)

I take myself to be accountable to the feminist philosophy community in all its intersectional glory, to our allies in critical race theory, disability theory, LBGTQ theory, and other forms of inquiry motivated by social justice concerns, as well as to philosophers interested in the social world or metaphysics more generally. This is a tall order, and I'm likely to come up short in various ways. I would, however, like to address a couple of methodological issues.

The first methodological issue is my use of examples. I was brought up in analytic philosophy where the use of abstract, even "cooked-up", examples aims to strip away all aspects of the situation that could derail us from seeing the main point or distinction under discussion. But such abstract examples may not be particularly apt when we want to show the efficacy of a particular theoretical apparatus in highlighting some real-world phenomena. Perhaps in those sorts of cases, using actual examples may work better. I do a little bit of both in this work.

The second methodological issue concerns the type of work it is. It is a work in metaphysics and in social theory. I am offering a framework, and the usefulness of that framework for understanding our social world ultimately rests on the application of it to various actual cases. I discuss some such applications, but they are mere sketches, and would need to be filled out in full empirical detail before a final verdict could be made.

The theory presented here lies at the intersection of metaphysics, social philosophy, social ontology, and feminist theory. Camping out at that intersection can be a lonely and cold endeavor: your metaphysics friends think our job is to describe the fundamental structure of reality and the social cannot be fundamental; your social ontology friends simply want to describe social reality in an entirely value-neutral way, unhindered by any political commitments; and your feminist and social philosophy friends either think metaphysics is an ideological part of the oppressive regimes we are fighting against or simply unnecessary baggage. I want to convince them all that there is material here worth engaging with. I have my work cut out for me.

CHAPTER 1 | The Conferralist Framework

1.1 Conferred Properties

In *Euthyphro* (Plato 1578: 10a), Socrates asks the dialogue's namesake,

> Is the action pious because it is loved by the gods or do the gods love the
> action because it is pious?

At issue is the nature of the property *being pious*: is it dependent on the
gods' love or not? For a moment, Euthyphro maintains that it is so dependent and that the action is pious because it is loved by the gods, as
opposed to the other way around. Socrates, of course, insists that being
pious is independent of the gods and their affections; they merely detect
a property the action already has and, upon detecting it, come to love it.

This disagreement concerns the metaphysical status of the property of
being pious: What kind of property is it? How independent is the property from the attitudes and practices of the gods? While our interest in
the Greek gods and their emotional lives has been replaced by interest in
humans and their own creations, the modern question of the metaphysical status of the various properties that clothe our world mirrors exactly
the Euthyphro question: What kind of property is the property of being a
woman, being male, or being black? How independent are these properties
from human thoughts, attitudes, and practices? The Euthyphronic intuition above is that they are not independently given, but rather dependent
in some way on human thoughts, attitudes, and practices. The question
is *how*.

We can attempt to flesh out Euthyphro's initial idea in several ways: we
can say that being loved by the gods *constitutes* being pious; that being
pious is a *response-dependent* property, such that an object is pious just

in case it induces love in the gods; or that the property of being pious is *conferred* by the love of the gods. It is the last formulation that I am advocating as a helpful way of capturing the nature of social properties of individuals.

I hope the intuitive idea is clear. Let us look at some more examples before making the conferralist idea more precise. Consider *being popular*. We cannot be popular in isolation; in fact, our popularity is entirely dependent on other people's harboring certain feelings toward us—or, as I would put it, other people's harboring certain feelings toward us confers the property of being popular on us.

Some properties, like being popular, are obviously conferred; others are plausibly conferred, but bear a close relationship to some nonconferred properties with which they can easily get confused. Consider, for instance, some baseball properties, such as a pitch's being a strike. There is a physical property, which we can allow is nonconferred, of having traveled some trajectory from the fingers of the pitcher to the glove of the catcher. We may think that whether a pitch is a strike or a ball is not a matter of what that trajectory is, but rather of what the umpire judges it to be. If we do that, then we say that the umpire is attempting to track what the physical trajectory is, but that it is his judgment as to what it is that makes something a ball or a strike. We then hold that the properties of being a ball or a strike are conferred by his judgment.[1]

A conferralist account of the baseball properties of being a ball or a strike has five aspects:

Conferred property: what property is conferred; in this case being a strike, being a ball

Who: who the subjects are; the baseball umpire

What: what attitude, state, or action of the subjects matter; the umpire's judgment

When: under what conditions the conferral takes place; in the context of a baseball game

Base property: what the subjects are attempting to track (consciously or not), if anything; the physical trajectory of the ball[2]

---

[1] For readers not familiar with baseball, consider the property of being *offside* in football (soccer) or the feature of being *in* or *out* in tennis. In all cases, a referee makes a judgment about what the physical properties and facts are, and that judgment confers the football or tennis property on the shot or behavior.

[2] In earlier work, (Ásta Sveinsdóttir 2013), I have labeled this a "grounding property", but now I think that "base property" is more apt. It is important to note that the subjects' attempts at tracking the property may be unsuccessful.

On a conferralist account of the property of being a strike, there is no fact of the matter as to whether the pitch is a strike or not independently of the judgment of the umpire, but rather it is his judgment about the trajectory of the ball that confers the property of being a strike on the pitch. There is, of course, a physical fact about the trajectory of the ball, but that physical fact does not determine the baseball fact. The umpire's judgment confers the baseball property of being a strike on the pitch and in so doing creates the new baseball fact that the pitch is a strike.

1.2 Comparison with Constitution and Response-Dependence Accounts

There can be reasonable disagreement about the baseball case. Consider, for example, the fact that baseball fans might both say "the umpire made a mistake and called a ball a strike", and also "the inning was over after the batter got three strikes."[3] The former usage seems to suggest that the property of being a strike is independent of the judgment of the umpire, but the latter requires a conferralist account of the property. The seeming ambiguity in the usage and some other features of the baseball case make it relevant for our purposes here and useful to discuss before we turn our focus onto the social.

Let's consider first whether the other two ways of fleshing out the Euthyphro idea above, the constitution account and the response-dependence account, are good ways of accounting for baseball properties. For although it is not very plausible to hold that the property of being a strike exists outside the game of baseball, one could capture the ontological dependency at the heart of Euthyphro's initial idea by saying that the ball's traveling a certain trajectory (given certain conditions) simply *constituted* its being a strike. You may recognize this as John Searle's early formulation (1997:28): *x counts as y in c*.[4] It is worth comparing the conferralist account I am offering here to what I label a "constitution" account of a property as well as a response-dependence account, since those closely related, yet different, accounts of a property can both seem to be articulations of the Euthyphro idea and might seem reasonable accounts of social properties, all being accounts that attempt to articulate a certain kind of ontological dependency on human thought or practices.

---

[3] This example is due to an anonymous reviewer.
[4] I discuss Searle's more recent formulation later in the chapter.

Let's stick to baseball and the property of being a strike for the time being to get a sharp contrast among those accounts. On a constitution account of the property of being a strike, the formula is thus:

the ball's traveling trajectory T in context C counts as a strike

Note that on a constitution account of being a strike, a pitch is a strike even if the umpire does not recognize it as such. The activity of the baseball players on the field thus generates a lot of baseball properties and facts, and it is the umpire's job to try to detect these properties and facts that come into being independently of him and his judgment.

What I find unhappy about that way of thinking of baseball properties is that, in this case, the umpire's job is purely epistemic: he is supposed to discern what the baseball fact already is. This is unhappy for two reasons.

First: Why do baseball players and their fans accept such an imperfect method for figuring out what the baseball fact already is—why has baseball not gone the way of American football, where the tape plays an all-important role?[5]

Second: The result of the judgment of the umpire plays a fundamental role in the game of baseball, including how the game progresses as well as the explanations people give of what happens on the field. It seems odd to say that there are these baseball facts out there that play no role in the game, namely those baseball facts not detected by the umpire.

Both of these concerns about the constitution account of baseball properties translate directly to the social cases, which we will get to shortly.

While I say that there is room for debate in the baseball case, I think the conferralist account of baseball properties is preferable, for the reasons I indicate, but my main objective isn't to convince the reader of conferralism about baseball properties, and nothing hinges on it for the social case. In particular, the "room for debate", mentioned earlier, does not carry over to the social case. The ambiguity in the linguistic usage noted above shows that there are two kinds of property in the vicinity in the baseball case. Conferralism offers one way to analyze the apparent conflict suggested by the linguistic evidence. On the conferralist account, strikes and balls are institutional properties conferred upon pitches as the umpire exercises his judgment as to the physical trajectory of the ball.

---

[5] Note, though, that even in American football, it is the judgment of the umpires upon seeing the tape that matters. The tape itself is inert and needs interpretation. The umpires' judgment provides that.

Conferralism can make sense of the idea that the umpire made a mistake, although on that view the umpire didn't make a mistake about whether the pitch was a ball or a strike, but about what the physical trajectory of the ball was. He judged it to be within the strike zone, say, but in fact it wasn't. He cannot, however, be wrong that the pitch was a strike, since his judgment as to the physical trajectory conferred that property onto the pitch.[6]

The constitution account offers another way to analyze the conflict over the linguistic evidence. A pitch is simply a strike if it meets the physical conditions for being a strike. The constitutionalist has to then make a distinction between two kinds of baseball properties: those detected by the umpire and those that go undetected. Only the detected ones play a role in the game itself. And the inning is over after the batter gets three *detected* strikes.

Both attempts to analyze the baseball case, the constitutionalist and the conferralist, involve some things that may seem unintuitive. The constitutionalist has to make a distinction between detected and undetected baseball properties and facts, and the conferralist has to say that the umpire, while he can be mistaken, cannot be mistaken about whether the pitch was a ball or a strike. This is why I say there is room for debate, because I think each can make sense of the baseball case, but each story involves some things that may seem unintuitive to some readers.

Why does this "room for debate" not carry over to the social case? The reason is simply that to give a metaphysics of social properties is to give an account of the properties that *do matter* socially, not ones that *should matter*, but don't. Similarly, were we to be offering an account of the properties and categories that do matter in the baseball game, as opposed to the properties that meet the conditions to matter, conferralism would also be a preferred account of the properties in question.

Whether the reader agrees with me about baseball properties is not all-important. What matters is that the difference between these two accounts of property be clear. It would make me even happier if the reader were to agree that there might be cases that are analogous to the conferralist account of baseball properties, namely where there is a physical property (or some other property not conferred in that context) in the vicinity that the conferrers are attempting to track, even though the property that matters is the conferred property itself.

---

[6] Cf. Gideon Rosen's (1994) discussion of the role of the judge who is judging the constitutionality of a law.

Let us also compare the conferralist account to a response-dependence account, where the relationship between the physical property and the baseball property is a *causal* one:

the pitch is a strike iff the ball's trajectory induces response R in umpire U in context C,

where the response in question is the umpire's judgment that the ball's placement is within the strike zone.

On a standard interpretation of a response-dependence account of a property, there is something in the object that *causally determines* the response in question.[7] On a conferral account, however, whatever there is in the object plays no causally determining role, only an epistemic one. There can be something in the object that the subject is attempting to track, but it does not induce or cause the judgment of the umpire.

The idea of a response-dependent property is that of a property that, while dependent upon responses of subjects, is grounded in some objective feature of the object. Many philosophers think that secondary qualities are captured by the idea of a response-dependent property because while nothing would be red, say, if there weren't subjects around to experience the sensation of having light that is reflected off the surface of an object hitting the retina in a certain way, the sensation that the subject has is causally determined by objective physical features of the object and the optical system of the subject.

I don't want to deny that physical features of the trajectory of the ball have a causal effect on the umpire (light reflected in certain ways, sound waves hitting the ear in a certain way, etc.), but I don't think that his

---

[7] The term "response-dependence" was coined by Mark Johnston in 1986 (cf. Wright 1992: 109) to draw a distinction between two types of *concept*. Johnston's main motivation for the distinction was to account for the difference between concepts of primary qualities, such as that of shape and size, and concepts of secondary qualities, such as that of colors and tastes. At the time, there was a renewed general interest in the primary/secondary quality distinction, and it also seemed that accounts of other qualities, such as aesthetic or ethical qualities, could benefit from a comparison with secondary qualities. Various writers have contributed to that discussion in some form or another, sometimes focusing on the response-dependency of *concepts*, sometimes of *terms*, but rarely on *properties*. I mention just a few works: Smith 1989; Lewis 1989; Johnston 1989; Wiggins 1976; McDowell 1983; McDowell 1985; Blackburn 1981, 1984; Pettit 1991. I will give a general characterization of a response-dependence account of a *property*, and disregard various issues regarding how to formulate response-dependence, as ultimately no such account is a promising account of social properties, as we will see later. There is one type of response-dependence account that might seem more promising, and that is the one where x is F iff x *merits* response R in subjects S in context C. Later in the book, I show that such an account is answering a different question from the one I am concerned with here.

judgment is causally determined by those features (plus his optical and auditory systems). On the response-dependence account of the baseball property, it is. On that account, for a pitch to be a strike is for it to causally determine the umpire to call out "strike", just as for a smell to be nauseating is for it to induce nausea in subjects. Subjects don't have any elbow room to respond in a different way to a response-dependent property; they respond in the way that they are causally determined to do. They are in fact physically compelled to respond in the way they do.

Moreover, if we want to maintain that the umpire can make errors of judgment as opposed to simply having a defective visual system, then the response-dependence account is not a promising account of baseball properties. Again, however, it matters little in this context which account of being a strike we opt for. The baseball case simply brings out the difference clearly. While the conferralist framework can be used to offer a conferralist account of any property, the plausibility of the account will depend on the kind of property it is and the details of the account. Our main concern will be, of course, how it fares as an account of social properties of individuals, and thus of the associated social categories.

1.3 Comparison with Certain Austinean Speech Acts

It is helpful also to compare the act of conferral to the more familiar speech acts of *exercitives* or *declarations* and *verdictives*, discussed by Austin, Searle, and others (Austin 1975; Searle 1969, 1979). On Austin's account of the speech act, when the umpire calls out "Strike!" he performs a *verdictive*. The verdictive class of speech acts are characterized by the fact that the agent is attempting to track an independent fact when making a judgment. Austinean *exercitives*, or what Searle calls "*declaratives*", on the other hand, are characterized by the fact that agents brings a new fact into being with their speech: *their saying so makes it so*. In paradigm cases of exercitives, there is no independent fact that is being tracked, such as when a judge issues a sentence after the prisoner has been found guilty.[8]

The act of conferral does not fit neatly into the framework offered by Austin and Searle, even if we restrict ourselves to acts of conferral that explicitly involve speech. The reason for that is that acts of conferral always result in a new feature being bestowed on something, and new facts come into being as a result. However, in the paradigm cases, it is also the

---

[8] This example comes from Rae Langton.

case that there is something that the conferrer is attempting to track. We can thus say that the acts of conferral by speech differ from the Austinean/Searlean speech acts in that they always have an exercitive dimension and typically have a verdictive dimension as well.[9]

Let me compare the act of conferral to verdictives and exercitives more closely. First, a conferral of a property may not take place with a speech act, although it can. But I think of speech acts that confer status onto someone as a subset of conferrals. If we look at Austin's taxonomy, exercitives confer status onto people, and, as will become clear, verdictives do so too, although Austin did not linger on that.[10] Rae Langton (2015) takes performing both of these as requiring some form of authority: practical authority in the case of exercitives; epistemic authority in the case of verdictives. I see the exercitives as requiring institutional authority, but the verdictives as being a heterogeneous set, where the paradigm cases, such as finding guilty or calling a penalty, require institutional authority but some other cases require only epistemic authority. Consider, for example, the case when you get your friend to diagnose a medical problem rather than a doctor or, again, a friend (perhaps even the same one) to value a painting you want to sell, rather than call an official appraiser. In the paradigm cases, however, you need to be playing the right institutional role in order to perform these actions. It's not enough that your friend consider you an epistemic authority. Moreover, in all cases, the authority you have needs to be recognized as well for you to be able to perform the action.[11]

Austin himself takes verdictives to have an obvious connection to truth and falsity, and when you call "strike" or pronounce someone guilty, the aim is to get things right. He even seems to think that disputes over verdicts show that the "content of a verdict is true or false", for example, when fans complain about an umpire's calls in baseball (Austin 1975: 153).

---

[9] I say, "typically", because the paradigm cases of the conferral of properties that explains the social categories all involve a verdictive element. The case of Nancy Milford's Sloane Square set might appear to be an exception, and I discuss it in chapter 2.

[10] Here is Austin's list of exercitives: appoint, degrade, dismiss, demote, excommunicate, name, order, command, direct, sentence, fine, grant, levy, vote for, nominate, choose, claim, give, bequeath, pardon, resign, warn, advise, plead, pray, entreat, beg, urge, press, recommend, proclaim, announce, quash, countermand, annul, repeal, enact, reprieve, veto, dedicate, declare closed, declare open. Examples of verdictives: acquit, convict, find, hold, interpret as, understand, read it as, rule, calculate, reckon, estimate, locate, place, date, measure, pit it at, make it, take it, grade, rank, rate, assess, value, describe, characterize, diagnose, analyze.

[11] Think of a case where the real judge has been kidnapped and locked in a room but storms in and says, "I find the prisoner guilty." Although they have institutional authority, it is not recognized, and the action fails.

A conferralist reading of Austin's verdictives class is such that what we have is two layers of facts, two layers of properties. There are the properties we are trying to track and the properties that get conferred. For instance, in the case of the baseball properties, the umpire is trying to track the physical trajectory of the ball. He can be wrong about what that is, but his judgment as to what it is confers a new property, a baseball property of being a strike or a ball. He cannot be wrong about whether it is a strike or a ball, but he can be wrong about what the trajectory of the ball was. Another person, I the fan, for example, can be wrong about whether it is a strike or a ball. I thought he called a strike, but in fact he called a ball, and, on the testimony of the person sitting next to me, I have to change my recording of the score in my notebook.

What a conferralist reading of Austin's verdictives makes clear is that verdictives involve the assignment of a status. This is in line with more recent work within the Austinean framework by Mary Kate McGowan and Rae Langton (McGowan 2004, 2009; Langton 2009) arguing that many verdictives have exercitive components. However, the conferralist framework can encompass both exercitives and verdictives and other acts that are structurally similar to verdictives, but that are not speech acts, and the emphasis is always on the assignment of a new status. In some cases, the conferrer is attempting to track an independent fact, in some cases not. In my application of the conferralist framework to account for social properties, the conferrers are always attempting to track the presence of a base property or properties, although I attend to a proposed counterexample to that shortly.

1.4 Social Properties

Let's go back to the social categories Solnit and Gómez-Peña experienced themselves as belonging to on their travels through San Francisco and their associated properties: Western, white, straight female, tourist from Argentina, the wrong kind of brown, older gay man, nobody. To say that they "experienced themselves" as belonging to these categories might seem to be skirting some issues, but I assure the reader that we will attend to them in due course. In particular, we will want to attend to how the account I develop does justice to how people experience themselves, while allowing for the discovery that one belongs to a social category. Likewise, the account will have to make sense of the idea that one can be mistakenly taken to belong to a certain category, as well as the phenomenon of "passing", where one actively encourages such mistaken identification. As is vivid in our story of Solnit and Gómez-Peña, different categories are salient in different contexts. Our account will also have to do justice to that observation. But all this is looking ahead. For now, let us simply attend to how to make sense of the metaphysics of the social properties of individuals: what is the nature of social properties? How does one acquire and keep a social property?

Social properties range in complexity and importance. We have mentioned a few already: being Western, white, straight female, tourist from Argentina, the wrong kind of brown, older gay man, nobody. Let us add to our list: being a woman, a redhead, male, black, married, queen, president, umpire, a university, a professor, surgeon general, a refugee, a radical, a Manchester United fan, a football player, a president of a football club, a popular footballer, a footballer's wife, a footballer's husband, a black footballer, a woman footballer. The list goes on. Some of the above cases may even strike the reader as not obviously social, but I hope that by the end of the story told in this book, it will be clear that they are so, too, after all.

Among social properties, it is important to distinguish between what I call "institutional" and "communal" properties. As you realize from the above list, many of these properties are not only social but institutional ones, and one's having the property in question is linked to one's place in an institutional structure. Perhaps the properties of being a queen, a president, and an umpire belong to that group. But perhaps some of the above properties strike you as not merely being a matter of one's place in an institutional structure. You may think, for example, that being a nobody, the wrong kind of brown, or a popular footballer are properties that aren't completely accounted for by pointing to one's place in an institutional structure. And even if one's place in an institutional structure plays a role in whether one has the property or not, one may think that the constraints on and enablements to one's actions aren't simply a matter of one's place in that institutional structure. This requires that we distinguish clearly between institutional and communal properties, even if both can be brought under the conferralist hat.

Searle has offered a very powerful and influential account of the construction of social reality, and looking at his account will help us distinguish between these two kinds of property.

As is well known, Searle draws on his development of J. L. Austin's account of speech acts (Austin 1975 Searle 1969, 1979, 1983) to offer an account of the construction of social reality (Searle 1997, 2010). In the early formulation of his work (Searle 1997:28), the following simple formula yields powerful results:

X counts as Y in C,

where X has the status function Y in context C. The formula yields powerful results because it is so versatile, as we can see from the following examples:

1. A stone counts as a paperweight in the context of my writing desk environment.
2. A piece of metal and wood count as a knife.
3. A particular person counts as an umpire in the context of a baseball game.
4. A piece of wood counts as a queen in the context of a chess game.
5. A piece of paper counts as money in the context of regulated exchange of resources.
6. Two people who have exchanged vows under certain specified conditions count as married in the context of a particular country.

Acquiring a new status comes with enablements: the object or person can do things or be something they couldn't before. In the case of agents, it also comes not only with rights and privileges, but with duties and responsibilities.

With this simple formula, Searle can make sense of the construction of our ordinary objects out of materials in the environment,[12] of the construction of art objects, as well as the construction of social entities and facts, which is his main aim. It all comes down to an entity or person's acquisition of a status and a framework for making sense of what having that status in a particular context means.

It is now time to articulate more clearly the distinction between institutional and communal properties. While Searle speaks in terms of social and institutional "facts" and "objects", I think I am true to the spirit of his account when I describe him as offering a constitution account of the various properties or statuses that concern him: being money, married, queen, president, umpire, university, professor, surgeon general, and so on. What our collective acceptance does is ground these statuses in

---

[12] I will not take a stand here on whether Searle manages to start with a base layer of brute facts out of which everything else gets constructed in a hierarchical manner.

some *authority*, and the constraints and enablements that come with the statuses in question become very distinct constraints and enablements, namely: rights, privileges, responsibilities, and duties. These are *deontic* constraints and enablements.

While I think that the conferralist account is preferable to Searle's constitution account for reasons I discuss shortly, I think Searle does very well in accounting for the social categories we find ourselves in, where the status or property in question is really an *institutional* status. Many of the categories we live with are like this: professor, student, citizen, legally married, renter, and so on. But many categories that we find ourselves in and that shape our lives are not institutional. We find ourselves thrown into categories by no one in authority, and often against our will. Yet we are constrained and enabled by our placement in these categories. I think of gender and, to a large degree, race as such categories. How are we to account for the metaphysics of those categories and the constraints and enablements that come with our place in them? I label this subset of social phenomena "communal."

The conferralist framework can handle both kinds of social property, institutional and communal. The model for the conferral of communal properties is structurally similar to that of institutional properties, but the conferral is not grounded in some authority. What is it grounded in?

It is helpful to again compare the conferral of social properties, both institutional or communal, with different ways to think about speech acts and the conditions for executing certain speech acts. J. L. Austin famously takes as a central case in his account of speech acts the case of marrying and getting married by uttering certain words such as "I pronounce you . . ." and "I do." If we focus on the case of the person who pronounces the couple married, we note that one of the conditions the pronouncer has to fulfill in order to perform the *exercitive* speech act of marrying is to have the authority to do so. That authority has, of course, been conferred on the pronouncer after certain conditions were met at some earlier date, but we need not linger on that. While this is a central case to Austin's account, there are other cases of speech act where it certainly doesn't seem to be the case that what enables persons to perform it is that they have the *authority* to do, even though they do need to have enough social *standing* to perform the action, such as when the school bully orders a kid to give him his candy on pain of being beaten up.

Consider the case when Billy the bully sees that Max's grandmother has given him the special candy from Austria, and says to Max, "Give me your candy!" Big-Tom, Big-Dick, and Big-Harry, Billy's posses, stand beside him, menacing. Max loves his Mozartkugeln and doesn't want to give Billy the candy, but he doesn't want to get the "toilet treatment" again. Although Billy does not have the *authority* to order Max to give him the candy, he has power over Max and can make his life miserable. This power is what enables Billy to *order* Max to give him the candy, even though he has no institutional authority over him. In this case, Billy's power over Max has its source in Max's fear of the things Billy could do to him. Billy, then, has enough *standing* with Max to be able to order him to give him the candy.

Sometimes the performers of the speech act possess neither authority nor standing themselves but rather invoke someone or something that does. In the context of talking about how slurs (racial, homophobic, etc.) get their force, Judith Butler (1993) discusses individual agents "citing" and "echoing" the authority of laws or other institutions, or the history of such laws or of discrimination and mistreatment. In fact, on Butler's account of speech acts, it is never the officials themselves who have the authority to confer anything on anyone, but rather it is their citing the authority of the law or institutions that does the work. She thinks that the force of a slur sometimes comes from citing the authority of laws and the like, but sometimes it comes from citing the history of a systematic injustice that may not have been encoded in law or explicitly embodied in institutions. More recently, Mary Kate McGowan has argued for what she calls "covert exercitives" and which she contrasts with the overt Austinean exercitives, where the speaker has authority (McGowan 2004). On her view, one is able to perform covert exercitives by being a participant in a norm-governed activity, and when an utterance counts as a move in that norm-governed activity, it is exercitive in that it changes what she calls "permissibility facts" for that norm-governed activity, that is, what is and isn't permissible as a next move. Participants are able to do this, even though they themselves do not have authority, because their utterance "triggers" the norms of the activity in question.[13]

I think we can learn a lot from the case of speech acts that can help us flesh out the conferralist story of social properties. In the institutional cases, the conferral is grounded in authority, in the communal cases in standing. I do not want to follow Butler and say that in the conferral someone or something with authority or standing is always *cited*, but rather allow that

---

[13] I am unclear about when something counts as a move and when not, and it seems that whether one is given the status as a speaker in that context matters to the question, but I will not linger on this issue here. The point is simply that there is an emerging literature on performing certain speech acts even when one does not seem to have (deontic) authority.

sometimes the subjects doing the conferral have authority or standing themselves. How the subjects acquire the authority and the standing is then an important question. The case when the subjects possess authority is relatively straightforward, since the subjects will have had the authority conferred upon them at some prior point. What about standing? What is the source of that?

Consider a US high-school cafeteria and the property of being popular, on the one hand, and being cool, on the other. Who are the popular kids and how do they come to be popular? The popular kids are popular because other kids like them. On the conferralist story, it is the other kids' liking them that confers the property of being popular onto the popular kids, and constraints and especially enablements come with it. This is power. The popular kids are able to do things others can't. They may, for instance, be able to determine who is cool or whose outfit is fashionable. They may decide that wearing black is the cool thing to do and whoever is wearing black is therefore cool, or they may simply like a particular person and their liking that person, in turn, confers the property of being cool on that person. Being cool comes with its own constraints and enablements. In the right context it too is power. The cool kids may be able to say or do things that others can't. They may be able to start a trend of dancing on tables or treating the custodial staff with respect.

Our example above is simple but suggestive. Being popular and being cool are conferred properties. They are social statuses consisting in constraints on and enablements to the bearer's behavior in the context. On the conferralist view, communal properties are conferred by subjects who have the standing to do so. In the case of conferring popularity upon someone, it is the others' sentiments that confer the status upon that person. You might wonder, Who exactly has the standing to confer popularity upon a person? The answer is that collectively, the others have to have enough standing (or sway) to confer the status. We can imagine a case of twenty people where fifteen of them like person A but four do not, but because the four have more standing collectively, A doesn't get the status of popular. So it isn't just a matter of the number of people. It is a matter of the standing of these people, individually and collectively. The standing itself can have its source in a variety of sentiments that others have toward the individual in question, such as fear, respect, pity, hatred, love, admiration, and so on; it may also have its source in a judgment to the effect that the individual has a certain property that is being tracked, such as wisdom or discernment. Communal properties or statuses themselves are then to be fleshed out in terms of constraints and enablements. These enablements are non-institutional powers, such as when the cool kids are able to lead the change the behavior toward the custodial staff in the school when others couldn't.

What about the cases where the conferring subjects do not possess the relevant authority or standing themselves, but seem to be citing it, as, for example, when the older sibling says to the younger that the parents have put a ban on eating Lucky Charms and thus the young one shouldn't eat it, or when the bully's posse has a private conversation with Max where he says that Billy the bully would like to have his candy? In the case of citing authority or standing, it is open to us to make sense of the mechanism of conferral by saying that the subject exercises the authority or standing *by proxy*, but we need not dwell on the details here.[14]

The conferral of social properties is a complex phenomenon. Some properties are conferred by subjects in authority, some by subjects citing authority. Some are conferred by persons who have standing, others by citing power structures that lack normative support. Some of those structures are backed by habit or inertia, others by the threat of violence. In the case of the conferral of communal properties, that is done in the context by subjects who either have standing or cite others who do. In addition, McGowan's suggestion, that people who are already participating in a practice can trigger the norms of that practice, can help us understand how people who do not have standing or authority can nevertheless help in maintaining oppressive communal practices or institutional structures by mere participation in the practice.[15]

On my view, then, a property P is an *institutional property* if it is a conferred property with the following profile:

Conferred property: P
Who: a person or entity or group in authority
What: their explicit conferral by means of a speech act or other public act
When: under the appropriate circumstances (in the presence of witnesses, at a particular place, etc); we can think of this as a particular institutional context
Base property: the property or properties the authorities are attempting to track in the conferral

---

[14] Kirk Ludwig's work on proxy agency may help us with this; see, e.g., Ludwig 2014.
[15] I say more about how individual actions contribute to structures of power in chapter 6.

A *communal property*, on the other hand, is a property P that is a conferred property of the following sort:

Conferred property: P
Who: a person or entity or group with standing
What: their conferral, explicit or implicit, by means of a attitudes and behavior
When: in a particular context
Base property: the property or properties the authorities are attempting to track in the conferral, consciously or unconsciously

Obviously, the above are schemas that need to be filled in for each property, institutional or communal. Let us do so for paradigm cases of an institutional property and a communal one, being elected president and being cool, respectively, that I mentioned at the outset.

First, let me fill out the details for the institutional property of being a president, taking as an example being elected the president of the United States:

Conferred property: being elected president of the United States[16]
Who: the current US vice president, as president of the US Senate; this is the entity in authority
What: the declaration that someone has received the most electoral college votes for US President
When: on January 6, following a November election, starting at 1 p.m.
Base property: the majority of electoral college votes, that is, 270 or more

Let me also fill in the details for the radically contextual communal property of being cool:

Conferred property: being cool
Who: the people in the context, collectively
What: their judging the person to have the base property or properties

---

[16] There is the complication that the elected president then has to *assume* office by taking an oath. Similarly, for other institutional offices, the person who has the status conferred upon them has to assume the role for it to fully take effect.

When: in a particular context the person travels in, for example, one context can be at Mission High School in San Francisco, another the skate park in the Sunset District of San Francisco; someone can be cool at Mission High, but not at the skate park

Base property: the property or properties the conferrers are attempting to track in their conferral in each contexts; for example, having blue hair may be a base property for being cool at Mission High; having a tattoo at the skate park

What is a context for our purposes here? Intuitively speaking, the context is the situation framing the encounter that gives meaning to the acts performed and enables the performing of those acts. There has been considerable work on context in philosophy of language, and there may be several ways to flesh out what a context is that may work for my purposes here. As Stalnaker's framework is intended to capture the dynamics of conversation in which speech is context-dependent action, his notion of context might provide a good analogy for the type of notion of action contexts we need here. Stalnaker (1999: 98) defines a context as "the body of information that is presumed, at that point, to be common to the participants in the discourse." This means that each conversational move changes the context, if only a little bit. If we helped ourselves to an equivalent notion of an action context, then we would say that the context is the body of information assumed to be common to the participants in the encounter. The use of "information" is a little unfortunate here, for it can include assumptions about what social map is operating in the encounter. I say more about social maps in chapter 6, but a social map consists of assumptions about what features of individuals matter to the encounter and what is associated with having such features. While I don't want to identify the action context with a body of information (I think of that as a category mistake), I take the reach of the context to be equivalent to the reach of the social map, and I think of the context as *associated* with the body of information.

My proposal is that the conferralist framework is a good way to account for social properties of individuals. The conferralist schema, when filled out, is a way to articulate the idea that we have a social property because of something about other people by saying that a social property is conferred upon us by other people. I think that it aptly captures paradigm cases of social property, such as being elected president and being cool. It does not do justice to the property of having red hair, a paradigm case of a property that is not social, as one does not have red hair in virtue of the sayings or doings of other people, but precisely irrespective of those.[17] Either the hair reflects light of a certain wavelength onto our retina or it doesn't.

Before discussing why I think conferralism is preferable to alternative accounts, let me address an issue concerning the details of the conferralist account. This is a version of the Socratic worry expressed earlier in the *Euthyphro* (7e): what if the gods don't agree? Our version of the worry is: What if the subjects doing the conferring don't agree?

When it comes to the conferring of social properties, the fact that the conferrers don't agree can take different forms.

In the first type of scenario, the group of conferrers don't agree, but the people among them with the most standing do, and they manage to confer a status.

In the second type of scenario, the people with standing disagree among themselves, so the group doesn't manage to confer a stable status onto the person. They may then be treated differently by different people, and there is no conformity that corresponds to the person's social status in the context. This is not a flaw of the account, in my view, as I think that accurately reflects the messiness of many of our interactions.

What should I say about the possibility of self-conferral?[18] In the case where persons have the authority or the standing, they can self-confer, and sometimes do.[19]

1.5 That Conferralism Fares Better Than the Constitution and the Response-Dependence Accounts

When attempting to account for communal properties like being popular, a witch, or a woman, I think it is not mere membership in a set of objects defined by the presence of a natural or legal property that matters, but the perception of others that the person has that other property. And it is not merely that the presence of some feature causes the behavior of other

---

[17] This is, of course, consistent with its being the case that in some contexts having red hair serves as a base property for the conferral of a social status, *being a redhead*, consisting in constraints and enablements, institutional and/or communal, as has been the case historically and persists to this day.
[18] Thanks to Abigail Klassen for pushing this point.
[19] The possibility of self-conferral means that one does not have social properties entirely because of other people, even though the availability of social maps, of course, depends on what has happened in other contexts in which one has traveled, and most of those are going to be contexts in which self-conferral was not possible.

people to be a certain way, but that those other people *judge* or *take* that feature to be present. Perception matters in the institutional cases as well, a key one being the perception at the time of the explicit conferral of the institutional property. That it is the perception that the particular feature is present that matters is captured by the conferralist account, and that is a crucial difference between the conferralist account and the two other accounts mentioned earlier, the constitution account and the response-dependence account. As mentioned earlier, on the constitution account, it is the *presence* of the feature that matters, irrespective of the perception. And on the response-dependence account, the feature *causally determines* the response of the conferrer.

A response-dependence theorist treats social properties like nausea: something in that delicious-looking sandwich induces queasy feelings in you and causes you to puke. Likewise, features of people cause us to respond to people in particular ways, including pronouncing them married, classifying them, and treating them in certain ways.[20]

I think a response-dependence account of social properties is unattractive. Apart from reducing the social to a mechanistic world of stimuli and responses, which can, of course, be part of a robust research program, there is a specific problem for the response-dependence theorist who wants to account for social properties. This is allowing for the cases where people are misclassified. To go back to our earlier example of baseball, how can the response-dependence theorist accommodate the intuition that the umpire is wrong when he calls a strike? On the constitution account, the pitch is either a ball or a strike already, and the umpire can be wrong in his call. On the conferralist account, there is a fact of the matter as to what the physical trajectory is, and the umpire can be wrong about that fact, and in judging that fact incorrectly bring into being a new institutional fact, which is the baseball fact that the pitch was a ball or a strike. Neither of these options is available to the response-dependence theorist. The umpire is simply causally determined to either call a strike or a ball. Just as there is no sense in saying that I am wrong in getting nauseated by anchovies—it is merely a chemical reaction I'm having—so too is there no sense in which the umpire shouldn't have had the reaction to the pitch that he had.

---

[20] A variant of the response-dependence account focuses on the disposition to cause a certain reaction in subjects, but the argument applies equally well in that case. The issue is the direction of fit: the response-dependence theorist makes the object (the physical trajectory of the ball; the physical features of the person) the responsible party; the conferralist locates that responsibility in the subject (the umpire).

The response-dependence picture of social properties, like being of a certain gender, looks like this:

a person P is of a certain gender G in context C iff P induces response R in subjects in C

For example:

P is a woman iff P causes people to have a "woman-reaction" to P

This sort of account makes it impossible to make sense of misgendering (when someone is mistaken about a person's gender) and passing (when a person passes as a member of a certain category), as people's responses are completely involuntary and there is no room for any sense of "getting it wrong."

Because the response-dependence account cannot make sense of mistakes about social categories, I take it to be a nonstarter as an account of social properties of individuals.[21] A more serious alternative is a Searlean constitution account. Let me now argue that conferralism is better than a constitution account of social properties.

Let me first address the worry, which the reader may have, that it isn't so clear that Searle is really a constitutionalist after all, as opposed to a conferralist. How does X gain the status function on Searle's account? Is it simply that being X in C is enough to constitute being Y, or do agents of some sort have to confer the status of Y onto X? We may, in fact, wonder whether it is collective acceptance that confers the status function, and thus that Searle may be a conferralist after all, because Searle has in his later work substituted the simple formula with another that makes explicit what role collective acceptance plays (Searle 2010: 101):

We (or I) make it the case by Declaration that a Y status function exists in C.

But we would be mistaken. It isn't the case that Searle has in his later work clarified the formula to make explicit that he is a conferralist; rather, he has clarified that what sets the requirements for the status in each context is determined by our collective acceptance, which is quite different. Let me flesh this out. Consider:

---

[21] I discuss a different type of response-dependence account in chapter 5, one in which the thing in question is to *merit* the response.

1. X's meeting conditions K in context C constitutes being B (Searle's early formulation).
2. We collectively accept that X's meeting conditions K in context C constitutes being B (Searle's later formulation).[22]
3. S's judgment that X meets conditions K in C confers being B onto X.

In 1, it is simply not specified what sets the conditions for X's being B. It is left open what does, including whether it is human activity or nature or something else. In 2, what collective acceptance does is determine what X has to meet in order to be B. Then either X meets K or not, and the collective acceptance plays no role in making X B.[23] In 3, it is the judgment of S that confers the property of being B onto X, and S is guided by the requirements that X has to fulfill, but it is S's judgment as to whether X meets the requirements that makes X B or not. Neither 1 nor 2 has such a role to play for collective acceptance. Searle's view, both in its early and later formulation, is constitutionalist.

The above discussion brings out that there are two things that distinguish the conferralist and the Searlean constitutional account.

First, it is the *perception* that the base property (or properties) is present that matters on the conferralist account, not the *actual presence* of it, as on the constitution account. Call this the "perception" aspect of the conferralist account of social properties.

Secondly, the conferralist offers a story of the *acquisition* of the property, not just a story of under what conditions something has the property. Call this the "conferral" aspect of the conferralist account of social property.

Here it is helpful to introduce a recent distinction among social kinds, introduced by Mohammad Ali Khalidi (2013). While Khalidi thinks that all social kinds are attitude dependent in some way, attending to what kinds of attitudes are at work and toward what exactly can help distinguish among three kinds of social kinds:

1. Neither kind existence nor kind membership depends on attitudes of subjects toward the kind itself or its members, although these kinds depend on subjective attitudes about other things. For example,

---

[22] To use Brian Epstein's (2015) helpful terminology, our collective acceptance *anchors* the constitutive rule.

[23] Again, to borrow Epstein's (2015) terminology, we collectively *anchor* the *frame* principle, but we play no role in whether a particular meets the *grounding* conditions.

whether there are such things as recessions does not depend on whether anyone thinks there are, and whether something is a recession does not depend on the attitude of subjects toward the phenomenon in question.

2. Kind existence depends on attitudes of subjects toward the kind itself, but not kind membership. For example, on Searle's account, whether the kind money exists depends on the attitudes of subjects, but whether a particular piece of paper is a member of the kind money does not depend on anyone's attitude toward it, but rather on whether it meets the requirements for kind membership.

3. Both kind existence and kind membership depend on attitudes of subjects. For example, one might think that whether there are such things as cocktail parties depends on subjective attitudes, and whether a particular gathering is a cocktail party or not also depends on what people think about it.

Conferralism about social categories of people is committed to the claim that such social categories are of type 3 on the Khalidi scale, that is, both the existence of the corresponding category and membership in the category depend on subjects in the way that conferralism outlines. A Searlean account of social categories has social categories fit into type 2 on the Khalidi scale. As Searle is chiefly concerned with *institutional* phenomena, his commitment to the second Khalidi type of social kind is not surprising, although I argue below that it has certain unintuitive results. It does not fit well with phenomena such as recessions, nor with what I call "communal" phenomena such as races and genders.

Searle does not offer an account of communal properties, but we can easily see how a conferralist account would be preferable to a Searlean-inspired constitution account in the communal case. The reason is that in the case of communal properties like being popular, a witch, or a woman, it is not mere membership in a set of objects defined by the presence of a natural or legal property that matters, but the *perception* of others that the person has that property that does. The story of how the status is acquired thus clearly favors the conferralist account. That it is the perception that the particular feature is present that matters is captured by the conferralist account, and that is a crucial difference between the conferralist account and the constitution account. As mentioned earlier, on the constitution account, it is the presence of the feature that matters, irrespective of the perception.

The conferralist can offer a uniform account of social properties that covers both communal and institutional properties; a Searlean constitution account can make sense of institutional properties, but the communal properties demand a different treatment. But the argument for the conferralist account and against the Searlean one does not simply rest on the appeal to uniformity and the fact that the Searlean account cannot account for communal properties. I also think that the conferralist account makes better sense of institutional properties than Searle's account. This is so because perception matters in the institutional cases as well, a key one being the perception at the time of the explicit conferral of the institutional property.

Let's take a clear example of an institutional property, *being married*, and see how things look on each account. On the conferralist account, a person in authority confers the status of being married onto a couple on a certain occasion and in that conferral is attempting to track certain properties pertaining to their eligibility to be married. These base properties vary from jurisdiction to jurisdiction, but they can include not currently being married to someone else, being of a legal marrying age, not being a close relative of intending spouse, and so on. The marriage conferrer may judge the couple eligible based on their word or based on documents they provide. The conferrer then confers the institutional status onto them. The couple may in fact not meet the eligibility requirements, but if the marriage conferrer judges them to, they become married anyway and get the certificate of their new institutional status to prove it. To be married is thus not to meet the various requirements for being married, but to be judged by a person in authority to do so.

On a constitution account of marriage, a couple gets married if a person in authority pronounces them so and they meet all the requirements. A marriage in which the eligibility requirements are not met, unbeknownst to some of the parties, is a fake marriage. The couple may act married and live like that for seven decades, but they are not in fact married.

The reason why the conferralist story is more promising in this kind of case is that we are giving an account of the categories that *matter* to our social life. As I look at it, a social property, whether institutional or communal, is fleshed out in terms of the constraints and enablements, institutional or communal, on a person's behavior and action. To have the status in question *just is* to have the constraints and enablements in question.[24] On a constitution account, on the other hand, these constraints and enablements

---

[24] Even if the marriage gets later revoked or even annulled, that doesn't change the fact that for some time, even decades, the couple functioned socially as married. The couple was married during that time, even though they ought not have been. Thanks to Catherine Z. Elgin for this worry.

have to be separated from the status acquired, since a person may acquire new institutional powers (they are able to do things, such as file jointly for taxes, because they appear to be married), yet not have the institutional status in question (since they don't meet the requirements, they are in fact not married, although everyone treats them as such). And this separation between what they can do and what status they have needs a separate explanation. This "argument from fakes" is not a decisive argument, but points to the fact that if what matters most is to give an account of *what does in fact matter* institutionally and communally, as opposed to *what meets the requirements to matter*, then the conferralist account fares better. It also fares better on simplicity: a social status just is the constraints and enablements conferred onto the bearer.

Although I have clarified how a conferralist account differs from a constitution account, there is a version of a constitution account that might seem to be equivalent to the conferralist account. This is a version that builds a perceptual element into the account:

being taken to have B by subject S in context C constitutes being F

I said earlier that there were two main differences between a constitution account and a conferralist one: the perception element and the conferral element. The conferral element answers the question how one acquires the feature, and the perception element highlights that membership is also dependent on others' attitudes, not merely the criteria for membership. What about this special case? Do we here have a case where the difference from the conferral account is that the perception element is present and the conferral one missing and it fits into category 2 on the Khalidi scale? That seems implausible, for doesn't it seem that a constitution account that builds a perceptual element into the account also makes membership dependent on subjective attitudes, and in so doing builds it into the account how people acquire the feature? And, if so, then it also seems to be in category 3 on the Khalidi scale.

Let's thus step back from how membership is determined and focus on how the criteria themselves are. They depend upon something about subjects for both the conferralist and the perceptual constitutionalist, but for the latter they are grounded in collective agreement. Social properties thus exist because of collective agreement, and their content is determined by collective agreement, on the perceptual constitutionalist account. That story works better for institutional reality than it does for communal reality, as it is implausible to think that people have communal properties because of collective agreement. On the conferralist account, however, many of the criteria for institutional membership (i.e., the base properties) may be encoded in law and the like, and thus rest on collective agreement, however much removed, but the criteria for communal membership are not determined by collective agreement, but rather negotiated, consciously or unconsciously, by the conferrers in the context.

1.6 Using the Framework

While I am primarily interested in social properties of people, these are really a subset of the large set of social properties. Other entities besides people, including inanimate objects, groups, and institutions, can have social properties conferred on them. To illustrate the complexity of social properties, and the possible interplay of the institutional and communal properties, consider the following fairly innocuous case of the various social properties involved in getting permission to park one's car on a city street and getting a ticket for a parking violation.

Consider the parking of your car in a contemporary US city like San Francisco. We can assume that the guiding idea behind parking regulations is that residents in the city of San Francisco who own a car are entitled to park their car in the vicinity of their home provided there is space on the streets and certain other laws are followed. But how does this guiding idea get expressed in a rule, and, in turn, how does the rule get implemented?

The way the idea gets expressed in a rule is that residents are entitled to a parking sticker to put on their car, provided they show up with certain documents that count as proof to the effect that they reside at a certain address and they are the registered owner of the car to which the parking sticker is assigned.

A person who show up at the parking office may in fact not be the owner of the car and may in fact not reside at the address indicated, but if they have documents to the effect that they do, that is what counts. The parking office personnel judge the documents presented as proof of ownership and residency, or not, and on the basis of their judgment, the applicant gets conferred the status of resident and car owner in San Francisco for the purposes of resident parking. Then they get issued a parking sticker, which they attach to their car, and off they go, parking away.

Once the car has a parking sticker, that is all that matters from that point on. Whether a car is entitled to park in a certain spot or not depends on whether it has a sticker of the right kind, not who owns it, drives it, or resides in the vicinity. For instance, it does little good to insist that one is the owner of the car and one lives in the house, outside of which the car is parked, in the face of a parking meter worker who is in the middle of writing up a citation of a parking violation. Similarly, one may have bought a car from someone who lived on a certain street and because the car has a sticker that is valid throughout the year, one can park one's car in the neighborhood of the former owner while the sticker is still valid.

We can say that the guiding rule for resident parking gets expressed by the parking office personnel conferring the institutional status of *having a valid sticker* on a certain car on the basis of the presumed owner's documents. When a parking meter worker issues a parking violation, they do so by judging that the car that is parked in a certain spot is lacking the institutional status of *having a valid sticker* and on the basis of that judgment, confer the status of *being in violation of parking rules* on the car.

This case illustrates that there can be hierarchies of institutional statuses, and whether one has a certain status in a particular context may depend on the conferrers' judgment of whether you have a status that is lower in the hierarchy, but how you got that status is irrelevant from that point forward. In this way, although we have a hierarchy of statuses, the whole thing does not crumble even though some status lower in the hierarchy was acquired by mistake or nefarious means.

Let us now introduce some communal properties. Let's say, for example, that there is a stigma associated with a car's having a parking violation, as evident by a piece of paper on the windshield. And let's assume further that the owners and drivers of such cars get treated with great suspicion. Let's assume, for instance, that I walk into a restaurant and apply for an advertised dishwashing job, parking my car outside the restaurant where it is in clear view of where I am being interviewed by the manager. My interview goes really well and I am about to be offered the job when the manager sees that my car has a parking violation ticket on it. Immediately the manager grows suspicious of me and my reliability. After all, there is a widespread belief, in this hypothetical scenario, that people who violate parking regulations are not to be trusted, not only for things to do with driving and parking, but for other matters of responsibility. After all, parking violators are, in this scenario, widely assumed to be a group of people who defy civic order and don't uphold community standards. The manager bids me farewell politely, and I am out the door without the dishwashing job.

This is a case where getting a parking violation is socially significant in such a way that persons who are taken to be parking violators get conferred on them a communal property, that is, their behavior and actions are subject to constraints (and enablements) that are communal, and over and above the constraints and enablements that come with the institutional status of being parking violators. Here we have the phenomenon that I will devote the next chapter to: a property that becomes socially significant in a way that generates constraints on and enablements to a person's behavior and action that are over and above the constraints and enablements that come with simply possessing that property.

1.7 Conclusion

We now have the building blocks for answering the questions generated by the story of Solnit and Gómez-Peña: What is the nature of social properties? How does one acquire and keep a social property?

On the view advocated here, a social property is a property that depends on other human attitudes and practices in a particular way, namely, it is conferred by human attitudes and practices, and that is how one acquires them. They are conferred onto us in the contexts we find ourselves in. We need to distinguish two kinds of social property, institutional and communal, where what grounds the conferral of the former is some authority, and the latter is social standing. Communal properties and categories are of particular concern to me in this book because these are properties and categories that are grounded in non-authorized standing and often involve the use of non-authorized power, including coercion, and this is rife with injustice, unfairness, and oppression.

Let me now turn to how institutional and communal categories are constructed, which requires us to articulate a particular conception of social construction that I call "social construction as social significance."

CHAPTER 2 | Social Construction
as Social Significance

2.1 Introduction

When we philosophers talk to colleagues in other humanities disciplines or the social sciences, we frequently encounter claims to the effect that a particular human kind or category of person is socially constructed.[1] A large number of philosophers dismiss such claims as resting on a confusion between the epistemic and the metaphysical: even though our conceptions of the category in question are shaped by social practices, that does not show that the category itself is (Boghossian 2006; cf. Hacking 1999: 28–30). And it is hinted that surely no one would want to put forth the metaphysical claim. Why? Because it is clearly false? Because it is confused?

This is the challenge I take up in this chapter. The aim is to discuss the various ways in which human kinds can be socially constructed, where that is understood metaphysically, and then to isolate a conception of social construction that is emerging as I articulate my account of social categories. I call this account "Social Construction as Social Significance", as it is an analysis of what it is for a feature of an individual to have social meaning.

2.2 Debates over Social Construction

The debate over the social construction of human kinds evokes earlier debates in the history of philosophy over the dependency of objects,

---

[1] I use the terms *kind, type*, and *category* interchangeably in this book, and there is no more to a kind than having a property that defines the kind or type.

properties, and kinds on human thought and practices: realism/conceptualism/nominalism on the one hand, and realism/idealism on the other. Allowing ourselves the broad strokes, we can say that the realism/nominalism debate concerns existence, and the realism/idealism debate the nature of that which exists,[2] although these issues overlap in various ways. While the question of the metaphysical status of human kinds concerns the reality of these kinds, a host of complicated issues gets brought together under that hat. Recent work on the metaphysics of social kinds has started to pull apart the various issues involved, but, with the notable exception of Ian Hacking's and Ron Mallon's work, this work has tended to focus on the reality of a particular category, such as race or gender, with no obvious upshot for the metaphysics of social construction generally speaking, or of human kinds in general.[3] It is, however, my explicit aim here to offer a general metaphysical framework that can support social constructionist claims.

A notable exception in the literature on human kinds is Hacking's work. Hacking has in his numerous articles and books offered a metaphysics of human kinds in general, and not just an account of a particular category or categories. The metaphysics he offers, dynamic nominalism about human kinds, is focused on existential commitment, and other philosophers have since been inspired by this framework and have offered a dynamic nominalism of a particular kind or category (for example, Sundstrom 2002).

Hacking's dynamic nominalism captures very well certain social constructionist aims, notably the commitment to the *noninevitability* of the kind in question, to *historicism*, and to the respect for *alterity*; this is in line with his intention to articulate a metaphysics for new historicism in history and literary theory (Hacking 1990). There are, however, other aspects of constructionism that dynamic nominalism, by itself, seems not to address.[4] In particular, an important aspect of the debate over the social construction of a particular kind or category is that it is a deeply political debate where it appears that its normative upshot is to follow from the metaphysical

---

[2] By saying that the realism/idealism debate concerns the nature of what exists, I don't mean to invoke the notion of essence or essentialism, but rather to point out the concerns with revealing the hidden nature of the thing in question. An example of this is to reveal something to be social when it is thought to be natural, or to show something to be normatively infused in different ways than is recognized. The kind of idealism that I have in mind is more Hegelian than Berkeleyan.

[3] Notable work here includes Alcoff 2006; Appiah 1990, 1996; Butler 1990, 1993a; Haslanger 2012; Mallon 2016; and many others. For bibliographical references, see, for example, Haslanger and Ásta 2017; James 2011; Mikkola 2016.

[4] For a discussion of the limits of Hacking's account of social construction, see Haslanger 2003, 2012.

status of the phenomenon. It seems, then, that a metaphysics of social construction should explain these normative implications, or show them to be in error. It is with this as a guide that I turn to the other side of the question of the reality of human kinds, the one that is not focused on existential commitment, but on the nature of the kind in question. The conception offered here is thus not in tension with Hacking's dynamic nominalism, but is designed with different constraints in mind.

The other notable exception is Ron Mallon's work, whose main aim in offering an account of the social construction of human kinds is to show how human kinds can play their rightful role in social scientific explanations. Both Hacking's and Mallon's accounts are designed with different constraints in mind than mine, and I discuss their views and how they differ from mine later in the chapter.

Let me focus on the constraints and aims of my account. As Sally Haslanger (2012) has discussed, an important social constructionist aim is to debunk widely held beliefs that function to justify oppressive arrangements, institutions, or practices. The beliefs in question concern the nature of the kinds or categories underlying these phenomena and are thus metaphysical beliefs; the debunking work consists in exposing the beast for what it is. A paradigm case of such a debunking project is to reveal a kind or category as a social category when it is widely held to be a natural one. The consequences of this are that the constraints and enablements that come with membership in the kind are then revealed to need justification; these constraints and enablements are shown not to be the result of some natural order of things, beyond the demand for justification.

Why would such exposure of the nature of a kind or category serve the political aims of fighting oppression? It does so by revealing the categorization and related arrangements as needing justification, when it had appeared that they simply were the product of nature, where a demand for justification was inappropriate. It is here that the normative upshot of the battles over social construction becomes quite clear. Showing the normative nature of a particular kind is a first step in exposing the values expressed in the arrangements, institutions, and practices involving the kind. It is these values that need to be examined critically.

Not all debunking projects involve revealing a kind to be social that is widely believed to be natural. Sometimes a kind is widely believed to be social, so that is not the erroneous belief in question. Instead, the widely held but erroneous beliefs concern the nature of that social kind and the justification of the constraints and enablements that come with membership in the kind. So, although some social constructionist projects involve showing a category or kind that is believed to be normatively inert to be in fact infused with a value that is in need of justification, other projects don't have that feature, but rather concern the beliefs about the particular normativity in question.

For this reason, I choose to describe a social constructionist debunking project in a slightly different way from the characterization above and say that the aim of the debunking theorist is to reveal which property is operative in a context. Understood in this way, the widely held but erroneous beliefs concern which property is operative in a context, and the debunking consists in revealing that some other property is really operative in the context from the ones that are widely held to be operative. This characterization departs in some ways from Haslanger's, but is, I believe, in the same spirit.[5]

It is commonplace in the humanities and social sciences to claim that something is socially constructed, but what does that really mean, and what consequences can be drawn from that? Sometimes the claim is that our social practices influence the way we think about something, but a more radical claim is that the thing is itself socially constructed. I first give an overview of social construction claims with particular attention to the latter type of claim. I then introduce a particular conception of social construction, which I maintain can help us understand the social construction of gender, sex, race, and other social categories, and aid us in the debunking project mentioned.

2.3 Causal Construction

There are many types of social construction (and hence, social construction claims). The first distinction we need is that between the epistemic and the metaphysical: Is it X itself that is socially constructed, or is it our idea or conception or knowledge of X that is? If the latter, then the claim that X is socially constructed is an epistemic claim in the sense that social practices are somehow implicated in our epistemic access to X. This is what Ian Hacking calls "idea construction" and which he discusses at length in *The Social Construction of What?* (1999:10). I will only discuss the types of social construction where X itself is supposed to be socially constructed.

---

[5] In fact, Haslanger (2012:370) speaks of "operative" and "manifest" concepts, although with a different distinction in mind.

I will first discuss causal construction and introduce the types of construction with a concrete example. Let's consider the claim, *disability is socially constructed*. This will, actually, turn out to be a host of claims, with varying implications.[6]

An individual has various physical features, and depending on the physical environment, can be more or less mobile within that environment. Let's say Sam can't walk and is a wheelchair user (S has feature W; S is W).

If the environment fits well the way the wheelchair works—there are smooth sidewalks with inclining curbs, all buildings are without thresholds and one story high, there is never any snow or flooding, and so on—then Sam can move around freely in his environment. If, on the other hand, there are some buildings that are taller than one story and without an elevator, then there are parts of the physical environment Sam does not have access to. We can call this a *physical consequence of being a wheelchair user, given the physical environment* (physical consequences of being W, given the physical environment).

But suppose it so happens that all parties take place on the second floors of buildings. No one intended it that way; it just happens. Perhaps it's a fad to have party venues with gorgeous views. The point is simply that no one intentionally picked second-floor venues because it would exclude anyone; no one really thought about it very much.[7] But the consequences are that Sam cannot go to parties anymore, and now there are not only physical consequences of Sam's being a wheelchair user, but social consequences of a certain sort as well. We can call this an *unintentional communal consequence of being a wheelchair user, given the physical and social environment*, following the distinction drawn in the last chapter. A meaner version of this is when someone, Kim, has realized that if she throws a party on the second floor, Sam cannot attend, and Kim deliberately decides to do so, to prevent Sam from attending. That case would be an *intentional*

---

[6] I discuss Elizabeth Barnes's account of disability in chapter 5, when discussing the application of the conferralist framework to the case of disability. I have chosen the example of disability because it is very clear to me that disability is socially constructed in all these ways, which may not be as clearly the case with all the other categories and features I discuss. In discussing my examples as I do, I do not mean to depoliticize disability. I am aware that the social and physical environment is profoundly ableist, but think that some of that can be captured by the interaction of the various ways in which disability is socially constructed.

[7] This may, in fact, have been the case before the introduction of the Americans with Disabilities Act (ADA) in the United States, which not only introduced legal protections, but also raised awareness.

communal consequence of being a wheelchair user, given the physical and social environment.

Suppose now that the voting booth is on the second floor of a building without an elevator, but no one had intended this.[8] Again, no one had given it much thought; it just sort of happened that way. While the voting commission is eager for as many voters as possible to take part in the election, some, like Sam, cannot vote. This would be an *unintentional institutional consequence of being a wheelchair user, given the physical and social environment.* And a meaner version of this is when some election officials have realized that if they put the voting booth on the second floor, Sam and others cannot vote, and they deliberately decide to place the voting booth on the second floor to prevent Sam from voting. That would be an *intentional institutional consequence of being a wheelchair user, given the physical and social environment.* We have, of course, many actual examples of this phenomenon, such as when polling places are only open during hours a certain section of the population cannot possibly make.

The types of consequences identified above can be lumped together under the heading *social consequences of having W, given the physical and social environment,* and the type of social construction in question we can call *social construction as social consequences.* This is a type of social construction Susan Wendell discusses in her "The Social Construction of Disability" in *The Rejected Body* (1990).

But social constructionist claims do not only concern social consequences of features or phenomena. Sometimes the physical environment gets changed as a result of social forces. Suppose that a certain kind of vehicle, The Hopper, gets to be very popular, and this type of vehicle requires very high curbs for parking. Then, in the absence of legislation pertaining to such things, curbs become increasingly higher in the area and formerly noncurbed sidewalks become not only curbed, but acquire very

---

[8] This example may not sit well with readers in jurisdictions where the law requires voting booths be wheelchair accessible, such as the United States, as it adds an extra institutional layer, namely the legality or not of the placement of the voting booth. We can alter the example to apply to an election in a private club, to strip it of the issue of legality. An actual example based on the US Supreme Court case of *Lane v. Tennessee*, provided to me by Anita Silvers, also illustrates the difference. In this case, John Wheelchair User is being sued in civic court by his landlord for making modifications to the entrance and bathroom of his rented house. The hearing is scheduled in an inaccessible courtroom in a building without an elevator. Case 1: the court clerk schedules the hearing for that upstairs courtroom, the usual one for such cases, thoughtlessly—he knows from the case that John is a wheelchair user, and he walks up the stairs every day, but doesn't put two and two together. Case 2: the court clerk has it in for John because he believes (mistakenly) that John is renting the house using Social Security income from other people's taxes, so he intentionally schedules the hearing in the inaccessible courtroom.

high curbs. This is a case of the popularity of a vehicle *causing changes* in the physical environment, and the type of social construction is *social construction as causal social construction*, much discussed by Hacking, as well as Haslanger and Mallon.[9] In our example, aspects of the physical environment itself, namely the curbs, are socially constructed in that social forces contributed to the existence or change in the physical features of the curbs. But since we are focusing on the example of the claim that disability is socially constructed, is this a case where disability is socially constructed as well? Yes, because any loss in mobility (and therefore increased disablement, given the physical environment) is a causal effect of the same social forces. Areas Sam could traverse freely before are now off limits, all because of the popularity of The Hopper.

This example brings out that although the type of social construction identified before, *social construction as social consequences of a feature*, is also a type of causal construction, it is helpful to distinguish types of causal construction by their locus: is the social phenomenon the cause or the effect? The causal construction discussed by Hacking, Haslanger, Mallon, and others is a construction where the social is the *cause*. In the first type discussed by Wendell, the focus is on the social *effects* of a feature. As we see in the above example, though, social forces can effect changes in the physical environment that can have physical and social consequences, so these types of construction interact in a variety of ways.

There is a special case, noted by Wendell, of the social causing changes in the physical environment with debilitating consequences. This is the type where social norms or ideals have the effect that certain bodies are not only abnormal, but disabled. When society is organized around what the normal or ideal is, that has a disproportionate effect on those who fall outside the norm. For instance, if public transportation is designed with four-feet-tall people in mind, then six-feet-tall people will have a hard time fitting through the bus doors and into the seats on the bus. Similarly, if the ideal of femininity involves being exceedingly thin and most clothes are designed around that ideal, then women who are not, who may even be the majority of the population, will have a hard time finding fitting clothes. There are two senses of "normal" at work here: the statistically normal and the ideal, and both can have the effect of marginalizing or making abnormal whomever they don't fit, with debilitating effects. This type of

---

[9] Hacking 1999, 2001; Haslanger 2012; Mallon 2003, 2004, 2006, 2013, 2016.

construction we can call *social construction as norms causing changes in the physical environment in such a way that having feature W is disabling.*

Finally, it isn't only the physical environment we interact with that can be changed as a result of social forces. Social forces can also cause changes in the physical features of individuals, making them physically impaired where they were not so before. We can have social forces (laws, regulations, corporations, community practices, etc.) that cause environmental pollution, which in turn cause debilitating diseases or restrict access to basic necessities, causing debilitating conditions in populations. In this case, social forces cause the very feature in question. We can call this *social construction as social forces causing feature W.*

2.4 Constitutive Construction

So far we have only considered causal construction. But not all types of social construction are of the causal kind. Sally Haslanger (2012) identified an important kind of construction, which she calls "constitutive construction", and which she defines as follows:[10]

> Constitutive construction: Something is constitutively constructed iff in defining it we must make reference to social factors.

Intuitively, X is constitutively constructed just in case social phenomena make up or constitute X. The notion of *constitution* is the familiar one: just as a material object is constituted by the materials that make it up, arranged in a certain way, so a social phenomenon is constituted by the phenomena (physical and social) that make it up, again, arranged in a certain way.

Haslanger first introduced constitutive construction to capture the kind of social construction going on in debunking projects. Examples of this are claims to the effect that sex or intelligence are socially constructed, when they are widely held to be a matter of biology. Another prominent example is the status of race, where a social constructionist argues that race is a social, and not a biological, phenomenon. And to continue with our example of the social construction of disability, a social constructionist would claim that disability is socially constructed as part of a debunking

---

[10] Haslanger 2012: 87. See also Mallon's slightly different formulation in Mallon ([2008] 2013):

X constitutively constructs Y if and only if X's conceptual or social activity regarding an individual y is metaphysically necessary for y to be a Y.

project: while it is widely held that disability is a matter of physical impairment, it really is a social phenomenon.

Now, to say that something is socially constructed constitutively can be a valuable intervention in a debate. The problem is that it doesn't say very much. We want to know how these things are constructed. And that's where different philosophical accounts of constitutive social construction come in. Haslanger has offered accounts of the constitutive social construction of gender and race. I want to sketch for you her accounts and tease out the account of social construction involved. My account is an alternative to hers. It is not just an account of race and gender, but of any social category. But first, Haslanger.

2.5 Haslanger's Account

Consider Simone de Beauvoir's words: "One is not born, but rather becomes, a woman" from the *Second Sex* (1953). This is taken to be the beginning of the distinction between gender and sex in feminist theory, which for American feminists, until Judith Butler, was something completely sacred.[11] On this picture, one is born biologically female or male and slowly becomes socialized into a woman or man. What is the relationship between sex and gender on this picture? The slogans used by feminists since the seventies are that *gender is the social meaning of sex* or *gender is the cultural meaning of sex*, and gender is thought to be a social construction.

Even though this marks the beginning of social construction talk, the social construction of gender is not a paradigm example of social construction in Ian Hacking's discussion in his numerous books, including *The Social Construction of What?* The reason he gives is that, in his view, the social construction of gender is not contested. Everyone thinks gender is a social phenomenon; everyone thinks it is socially constructed! All the more reason to give an account of what it is for gender to be socially constructed, one would think.

Haslanger embraces the slogan *gender is the social meaning of sex* and the analogous slogan *race is the social meaning of "color"*, and the conceptions of gender and race that she offers are to do justice to those slogans. While she discusses many ways something can be socially

---

[11] This is so even though Beauvoir scholars agree that Beauvoir herself did not hold the view attributed to her. See, e.g., Moi 1999; Bauer 2001.

constructed, a central conception of social construction she is aiming to articulate is one that makes sense of these slogans. Here are her accounts of gender and of race (2012:231, 236):

- S is a woman iff
    (i) S is regularly and for the most part observed or imagined to have certain bodily features presumed to be evidence of a female's bio- logical role in reproduction;
    (ii) that S has these features marks S within the dominant ideology of S's society as someone who ought to occupy certain kinds of social position that are in fact subordinate (and so motivates and justifies S's occupying such a position); and
    (iii) the fact that S satisfies (i) and (ii) plays a role in S's systematic sub- ordination, that is, along some dimension, S's social position is oppressive, and S's satisfying (i) and (ii) plays a role in that dimension of subordination.
- S is a man iff
    (i) S is regularly and for the most part observed or imagined to have certain bodily features presumed to be evidence of a male's biological role in reproduction;
    (ii) that S has these features marks S within the dominant ideology of S's society as someone who ought to occupy certain kinds of social position that are in fact privileged (and so motivates and justifies S's occupying such a position); and
    (iii) the fact that S satisfies (i) and (ii) plays a role in S's systematic privilege, that is, along some dimension, S's social position is privileged, and S's satisfying (i) and (ii) plays a role in that dimension of privilege.
- A group is racialized (in context C) iff (by definition) its members are (or would be) socially positioned as subordinate or privileged along some dimension (economic, political, legal, social, etc.) (in C), and the group is "marked" as a target for this treatment by observed or imagined bodily features presumed to be evidence of ancestral links to a certain geographical region.

Both genders and races are socially constructed constitutively. To be of a gender or a race is to have a place in a hierarchical structure, and genders and races are constituted by the hierarchical power relations. So here we have an account of constitutive construction: genders and races are constituted by hierarchical power relations. How does this do justice to the aforementioned slogans? To be of a certain gender, for example, is to be taken to have bodily features presumed to be evidence of a role in biological reproduction and be placed in a hierarchical power structure as a result.

2.6 My Account

I engage with Haslanger's accounts of gender and race later in the book; now I turn to the account of social construction that I offer as an alternative to her account of constitutive construction. My account can play a role in debunking projects, as we will see shortly, but its main role in this book is to explain how social categories of people are created and maintained.

My account of social construction also takes as central the type of social construction at issue in the feminist slogan *gender is the social meaning of sex*. I don't embrace that slogan, for reasons that will be apparent in the next chapter, but I want to capture that type of social construction. I label the conception of social construction I am articulating "social construction as social significance."

This is an entirely general account of social construction, in that I'm offering a conception of social construction of any feature F: the social construction of F as the social significance of a feature B, which serves as the basis for the conferral of F.

I will also say that for a feature F to be socially constructed involves the assignment of a social status, but the details and the mechanism of the account differ considerably from Haslanger's.

This is the idea: for a feature B to have *social significance* in a context is for another feature F to be conferred upon people taken to have B. F is then the socially constructed feature.

Let's take the example of disability again. For disability to be socially constructed, on this conception, is for a feature, physical impairment, to have *social significance* in a context such that people taken to have the feature get conferred onto them extra social constraints and enablements that are over and above the constraints and enablements that mere physical impairment brings. In effect, people taken to have the feature in question (here physical impairment) get conferred on them a social status, which consists in constraints on and enablements to their behavior. For instance, there can be institutional constraints, such as laws banning people with physical impairments from driving, even though the people in question could physically drive; or communal constraints, where no one takes what you say seriously because of the difficulty you have with articulating words clearly, even though you have epistemic authority on the matter at hand.[12] There can also be enablements. People taken to have physical impairment can be granted certain allowances, such as being permitted to park in certain designated areas, or to preside over religious rituals.

2.7 Social Construction and the Debunking Project

We have seen how the conferralist framework has been used in articulating a certain conception of social construction. Let us now see how this conception of social construction can be used in debunking a social constructionist project. To illustrate that the debate does not always concern the status of phenomena that are believed to be natural, let us consider, for example, the debate over whether refugees are socially constructed (cf. Hacking 1999; Haslanger 2003). In this debate, the social constructionist insists that being a refugee is not merely about being of a certain legal status. It is something over and above that, whereas the opponent insists that being a refugee is precisely and simply to be of that legal status. The opponent may even take a page out of Searle's book (Searle 1997) and say that having a certain legal status constitutes being a refugee. How can the conferralist framework and the newly articulated conception of social construction help us diagnose what is at issue here?

What we have here from the social constructionist's point of view are hierarchies of conferred properties. The institutional property of being a legal refugee is conferred on an individual by authorities, and with it come legal privileges and burdens. Both the constructionist and the anticonstructionist agree on that. The social constructionist, on the other hand, insists that there are also communal constraints and enablements that refugees face that are not direct consequences of the legal privileges and burdens that come with the legal status itself. These constraints and enablements can be explained by reference to the conferralist framework by saying that apart from the institutional (legal) property *being a refugee* that comes with legal privileges and burdens, there is also another conferred property *being assumed to be a refugee*,[13] which comes with its

---

[12] There are connections here with recent work on epistemic injustice, for example, Fricker (2007), although her analysis focuses on how the stereotype of the social group a person belongs to undercuts that person's status as a credible testifier. I see that case as a special case of a more general phenomenon. I will explore those connections at a later date.

[13] Sometimes the conferred property has another name, as in the case of gender, but often there is no other name used, which adds to the confusion. The legal status and the communal status are two

own communal constraints and enablements. In the conferral of this latter property the property *being a refugee* is the base property. As usual on the conferralist framework, a person can have the conferred property, yet not have the base property itself. But this is how it should be. The presence of the conferred property, not the base property, is what explains the social constraints and enablements the person is subject to in a context.

By using "hierarchies" here, I need not commit myself to there being an absolute hierarchy of conferred properties, only that in a particular context there can be a relative ordering of properties in the sense that one property is a base property in a context and another is the conferred property in that context. The base property of one context can thus be the conferred property of another.[14]

On my diagnosis of this debate over the question whether being a refugee is socially constructed, the constructionist and the opponent have their eyes set on different things: the opponent focuses on the legal status itself, whereas the social constructionist attends to the communal property conferred on individuals presumed to have the legal status. The debunking move consists precisely in exposing that the operative property in the context is the higher-level conferred property, not the legal property that is the basis for the conferral.

On the account put forward here, the social constructionist's debunking move reveals two things. The first is that membership in a certain social category comes with constraints and enablements that are not justified with reference to the presence of the property that is taken to define the kind. These constraints and enablements are as a result of a conferred status, and it is the conferral of this status (with its constraints and enablements) that is in need of justification. The second thing that is revealed is that the operative property in the context, the property that is responsible for the constraints and enablements in the context, is the conferred property, not the base property that the subjects of the conferral are attempting to track.

What is the political upshot of the social constructionist debunking project so described? It is not only that theorists can then ground their demand for justification of the distribution of privileges, burdens, and the like, that come with the conferral of the property in question; they also stand on firm ground when they critique it and ask related questions, such as who may be benefitting from the social arrangement. However, that a certain

---

different statuses, two different properties, and consist in different constraints and enablements, legal and communal.

[14] Thanks to Sylvain Bromberger for pushing me on this.

property has social significance may not always be unjust; it is a separate endeavor to examine it and show it to be so, even though, often enough, a social constructionist may be motivated to show that a kind is socially constructed precisely because the social significance of a property results in an unjust and oppressive arrangement.

2.8 Conferralism and the Explanation from Social Significance

A certain aspect of the account of social construction offered here may concern the reader. It is that the explanation of the social constructionist claim is that apart from the base property in a context—be it *being a legal refugee, being W,* or what have you— there is also on top of it this other property, the conferred property (*being assumed to be a refugee, being disabled,* and so on). Isn't there a danger of a proliferation of conferred properties? Why posit these extra properties? Why not refrain from introducing new social properties on top of the other ones, and instead simply say that the (base) properties in question are socially significant in a context and leave it at that?[15]

Let's try to flesh out this proposal. It seems at the outset to do justice to the post-Beauvoirean feminist intuition that gender is socially constructed in the sense that sex is biologically given and gender is the social meaning of sex. We want to flesh it out without adding some extra social property on top of sex; instead, we would simply say that gender is the social meaning of sex in a context.

But what would it be for a property to have social significance or meaning in a context? For something to be socially significant in a context is for it to play a social role, to have social meaning attached to it. For instance, we can imagine a context in which having a big nose has social significance, and other contexts where it plays no social role. In the context in which having a big nose has social meaning, certain privileges and burdens may come with having a big nose (for instance, job advancement); in contexts where having a big nose has no social meaning, nose size is not correlated with the distribution of resources, privileges, or burdens.

But how are we to capture the idea that a certain property has social significance in a context? Isn't the conferralist framework exactly one that

---

[15] I use "socially salient" and "socially significant" interchangeably in this book.

can give a precise formulation to this idea? For a property to be socially significant in a context is for it to be the basis for the conferral of another property, which brings with it constraints and enablements.

Let's take an example. Let's say that we want to flesh out the post-Beauvoirean position along these lines. Then we say that sex is socially significant and it manifests such that in a context another property—being of a certain gender—gets conferred on people presumed to be of a certain sex, and with this conferral come constraints and enablements.

The conferralist framework thus seems ideally situated to capture the idea that a certain property is socially significant and that the social construction of the associated category or kind consists in that. The proliferation of properties is not superfluous, but is indeed needed to explain social behavior by reference to the constraints and enablements that come with the conferred properties. The conferralist account does better than a constitution account such as Searle's, since the relationship between the base property and the conferred property is epistemic, that is, it isn't whether people have the base property that matters, but whether they are taken to have it. What matters socially is what features you seem to have, not what you do have, and this is well captured by the conferralist account.

What I am offering is a conception of social construction that is overlooked in the literature, even though it is of the same type as Haslanger is interested in capturing in her account of gender and race. She offers accounts of gender and of race, but in so doing offers accounts of what it is for sex and for "color" to be socially significant. My account is explicitly an account of what it is for any feature to be socially significant, and it captures an important aspect of the ways in which something can be socially constructed. It is an account of what it is for a feature of an individual to have social meaning and thus is a part of an account of social meaning. Social meaning, on this conception, is not about people's mental associations with the feature or group in question, but about what you can and cannot do (institutionally and communally) if you are taken to have that feature.

2.9 Constructing Social Categories

Now I want to address the question of how we can account for social categories, using this conception of social construction. The idea is that social categories, the categories we live by, are constructed by the behavior of individual agents, as they confer a social status on people taken to have salient properties in contexts. These social categories are the categories of people sharing a social status in a context.

As the conferralist framework can be used for many things, it is helpful to isolate the particular kinds of conferral actions involved in the construction of social categories. I choose to call the institutional version "classifying" and the communal version "placing". Features that are socially significant in a context serve as the basis for these types of conferral action: an institutional authority *classifies* persons based on some feature they are taken to have; and an individual or group with social standing *places* individuals into a social category that is a live option in a context on the basis of a feature they are taken to have. The placings actually allow for more complexity, and I attend to that in chapter 6, when I present an account of identity that accompanies my account of social categories.

But now two related worries arise.[16] One is my suggestion that social categories are constructed by means of these conferral actions, classifications, and placings. Doesn't it seem, rather, that social categories are created by means of Austinean exercitives or Searlean declarations, such as when the declaration is made, "Black people cannot vote" or "Jews cannot own property"? Relatedly, one may worry about my insistence that there is always some base property involved in classifying and placing and thus in the construction of social categories.

Let us consider the creation of categories first. There may be a certain amount of unclarity still in my use of "categories". I said at the outset that a category is a collection of entities or stuffs, united by a feature. Categories of people are collections of people who share a certain feature. Categories are not private mental entities, nor aspects of "cognitive architecture." Nor are they semantic entities.[17]

When it is declared, "Blacks cannot vote", what is brought into being are constraints that come with membership in the category Black. It is not an answer to the question what makes you belong to the category itself, but what the consequences of membership are for you. When it is declared "Jews cannot own property", nothing has been illuminated about what makes someone a Jew. Again, it is a specification of some of the constraints that membership in that category brings in that context, but does not tell us anything about what it is to be a Jew and how the categories of Jews are constructed.

---

[16] I am indebted to Rae Langton for these objections.

[17] Would a category of people exist in the absence of the people having the defining feature? This is the old medieval question of nominalism versus realism regarding categories, and nothing said in this book hinges on the answer to that question, so I will not address it here.

The above discussion brings out the need to distinguish two related questions: (1) What makes a person have a certain status? (2) What is the content of the status? I am primarily concerned with the first question in this book.

Let us turn to the other worry. Couldn't there be social categories where there isn't any base property people are attempting to track? And if there are such social categories, doesn't that show that the framework I'm offering is inadequate to the task, and at best only useful to account for a subset of social categories, the social categories that are the products of classifying and placing?

Consider, for example, the case of Nancy Mitford (1956), who wrote about the Sloane Set in Sloane Square in London. The Sloane Set decided what was U and non U (this is code for "upperclass"). Using certain words was U, others non-U. Using cloth napkins was U; paper napkins non-U. And so on. The Sloane Set decided these things, and was not attempting to track any independent fact, and yet, it would seem, people exhibiting U behavior were Us, and people exhibiting non-U behavior non-U. We thus seem to have the social categories of Us and non-Us, without any base properties involved in the conferral.

But this is not a case where there is no base property at all. For doesn't it seem that whether someone gets U status or non-U status depends on whether they are seen to exhibit the tastes of the upper classes? The tastes of the upper classes can change, of course, and someone can be keeping up with those changing tastes or not.

Us, then, are those who are taken to be keeping up with the changes in taste of the Sloane Square Set. The non-Us are those who are taken not to do so. The base property is this: is keeping up with the changes in Sloane Square Set tastes.

This is thus not a case of a counterexample to my account of social categories using the conception of social construction I proposed. Nor is it a counterexample to the claim that social categories are constructed through the acts of classifying and placing.

2.10 Comparison with Hacking's and Mallon's Views

2.10.1 Hacking's Description Dependence of Human Kinds

Ian Hacking (1999) makes use of Elizabeth Anscombe's ([1957] 1963) idea that intending something is acting under a description when he gives his account of kinds of people, or human kinds. The examples of human kinds that he is particularly concerned with involve ones that have been used in social or psychological analysis, such as child molesters, homosexuals, hysterics, and manic-depressives, but also ones that exemplify a particular culturally specific way of being, such as the Parisian *garçons de café*. His contention is, first, that one cannot be a member of such human kinds unless the concept of being such a person is available and, second, unless one intentionally acts in a certain way, which, following Anscombe, is to act under a particular description. This is part of his deeply historicist conception of human kinds, which means that kinds exist in their historical contexts but are not to be found also in other historical times and places that lack that historical specificity and the accompanying conceptual resources. Both his claims are controversial and in my view not sustainable without some further work. Could there have been homosexuals in ancient Greece, for example, before the nineteenth-century medical concept of the homosexual was available? If not, how do we make sense of the intuition that there have always been homosexuals, and on what basis do we base our solidarity with people across spatial and temporal locations? Here one might want to distinguish between two kinds of groupings of humans: a thin one that requires only that the individuals fit a certain description, and a thick one where it is a necessary condition of belonging to that kind that one think of oneself as belonging to that kind and act out one's conception of oneself as such. The *garçon de café* may be just such a latter kind, as well as other ones that involve specific historically situated ways of being in the world, as mentioned above. The other type of cases that involve psychosocial analysis may fall into the thin category, where what is at work is the classification of individuals by a third party, be it the state, doctors, or social scientists.

I have suggested that the cases Hacking discusses should be separated into two categories: those that involve a classification by a third party and those that involve self-identification. Following Foucault and Hegel, Hacking believes that the classification of human individuals always has a causal effect on those classified and that they have to respond to how they are classified (this is the "looping effect"). They don't have to embrace how they are classified—they can try to resist the classification or negotiate it—but they have to respond in some way. And often the response is at least a partial embrace of the classification. Why? Because often those classified are marginalized within the society and especially marginalized when it comes to conceptual resources to make sense of their own experiences, or what get called "hermeneutical resources", and the promise of a conceptual framework to make sense of those experiences is very tempting. For this reason, what was initially just a third-party classification of individuals may develop into a culturally specific way of being in the world that people can identify with and aspire to. Thus a "thin" kind can become a "thick" one.

So, on Hacking's conception, for a human kind to be a social human kind requires the availability of a concept of that kind, with an associated description. Can we extract a conception of the social here? Yes. A social kind is a description-dependent kind. Some kinds require that the description be something the members are acting under; others simply require that the description be available.

As the reader can see, there are some issues involved in fleshing out Hacking's idea that human social kinds are description-dependent, even if we restrict ourself to human kinds only. I will not settle the question here how well the theory can hold up to scrutiny, but rather point out that the conferralist constructivism I offer in this book does not require the availability of descriptions for a category of humans to exist. It does, however, require the presence of constraints on and enablements to the behavior of those taken to have the relevant base properties in the contexts.

2.10.2 Mallon's Social Role Account of Human Kinds

Ron Mallon's aim in his many papers, collected and expanded in his new book (2016), is to offer a social constructivist account of human kinds that can do the work that social scientists want and need for their explanations of social phenomena. He is thus motivated by different concerns than social philosophers and theorists who are motivated by social justice concerns (2016: chap. 9). I agree with him that the resulting accounts can be compatible, as they have different aims, and I think our accounts are largely compatible. The main differences that I see between his account and mine is that he takes social roles to be representation-dependent:

> A social role exists if and only if the following are met:
> SR1: Representation: There is a term, label, or mental representation that picks out a category of person C, and that representation is associated with—and figures in the expression of—a set of beliefs and evaluations—or a conception—of the person so picked out.
> SR2: Social Conditions: Many or all of the beliefs and evaluations in the conception of the role are common knowledge in the community. (2016: 58)

On Mallon's account, social categories are *entrenched* social roles, which are social roles that

> structure individual behavior on the part of both users of representations and those who fall under the representations . . . that lead to attendant changes in the environment—to the cultural networks, institutions, conventions, norms, spatial arrangements, and material environments that outlast individuals, producing standing circumstances that themselves feed back into the features of individuals (89).

Mallon then argues that entrenched social role categories meet Richard Boyd's (1999) requirements for being *homeostatic property cluster kinds*, which justifies their status as *explanatory*. I will not touch on whether Mallon's defense of entrenched social roles as fit for the sort of social explanation social scientists require is successful; I only point out where I see the main differences between his account of social role and mine of a conferred social status. The main difference, as I see it, is in Mallon's insistence that a social role only exists if there is a *conception* of the category commonly available in the culture. Here I think he sides with Hacking and Foucault in a version of description dependency. I think, on the other hand, that a social status can exist, even if people are not aware of their differential treatment of certain people. When a conception of the category is available, that signals the role of ideology in the entrenching of the category, where justificatory stories are offered for the differential treatment. But I think the status can exist in the absence of such an overt ideological role in its maintenance.

2.11 Looking Ahead

In the next chapter, we take steps toward using the theoretical machinery offered here to make sense of the construction of specific categories. The first categories we turn to are that of sex and gender, and I begin by discussing the dominant accounts of sex and gender in feminist theory the last few decades, the post-Beauvoirean one and that of Judith Butler.

CHAPTER 3 | Sex and Gender
| *From Beauvoir to Butler*

IN THE LAST chapter I offered a conception of social construction that was to capture the type of social construction at issue in the feminist slogan "gender is the social significance of sex." While I have been very influenced by what I call "post-Beauvoirean" feminist theory, I said that I did not embrace that slogan, partly because I have also been influenced by the writings of Judith Butler on sex and gender and related topics. For this reason, in this chapter I flesh out the conferralist interpretation of the status of sex and gender on the post-Beauvoirean picture and offer an interpretation and critique of Butler's accounts of gender and sex to set up my own accounts of gender and sex, which I put forward in the next chapter.

3.1 Introduction

Within feminist theory, the influence of the publication of Simone de Beauvoir's *Second Sex* (1949) is clear: Her remark "One is not born, but rather becomes, a woman" is not only interpreted as a commitment to a distinction between sex and gender, but also to the view that gender is a social construct and not determined by biology.[1] On the standard, albeit erroneous,[2] interpretation of Beauvoir's view, sex is a biological category and gender the social meaning of sex. More recently, Judith Butler has

---

[1] She did not coin terms for the categories of sex and gender, but by insisting that one is not born, but rather becomes, a woman, she can be read as implicitly drawing such a distinction.

[2] Any Beauvoir scholar will insist on this. See, for example, Toril Moi (1999) and Nancy Bauer (2001).

offered a recognizably metaphysical[3] story to support her liberatory political agenda (1990, 1993), where gender and sex are both social constructs
but their role is reversed: the schemas of gender determine what bodies and
body parts get sexed. The view that I offer of social significance and social
construction owes much to Butler, and hence I start by offering an interpretation of the metaphysical picture of sex and gender she offers as an alternative to the Beauvoirean one and to the radical linguistic constructivist.

3.2 Butler's Account of Sex and Gender: An Interpretation

My interpretation of Butler's views centers around four ideas. Firstly,
Butler offers a reorientation in the way in which the relationship between
gender and sex is to be thought. Sex is now to be thought of as materialized
through the regulatory schemes of gender, as opposed to gender being
the social significance of sex, as the post-Beauvoirean feminist theory
has had it. I appeal to the idea that what appear to be *assertions* of sex
are different sorts of speech acts, namely Austinian exercitives, to try to
capture that reorientation. Secondly, I appeal to an analogy with a game
to illuminate how the regulatory schemes of gender work to determine
meaningfulness. Thirdly, I appeal to Hegel's expressivist theory of the development of the subject and of objectification to cast more light on how
sex gets materialized on Butler's story. Lastly, I appeal to an analogy with
Kant's transcendental idealism to help situate Butler's story in the ontological landscape between the Beauvoirean position and the radical linguistic
constructivist one.

3.3 The Legacy of Simone de Beauvoir

As has been mentioned, it is with Simone de Beauvoir's *Second Sex* that a
distinction between sex and gender begins to be made in feminist theory.

Sex is taken to be a biological category, and *gender* the social significance of sex. For Beauvoir's followers, drawing the sex/gender distinction
had liberatory purposes, for the aim was to argue against the view that, to
put it rather generally, social reality was determined by natural reality. The
division of labor between men and women, and the inequality following

---

[3] Whether or not Butler herself considers herself to be doing metaphysics is not the issue. Theorists
can have a metaphysics even if they don't consider themselves to be doing metaphysics. Thanks to
Helen Longino for this point.

from that division, had been thought to have a natural justification in biology: women's biological features explained and justified women's place and function within the social sphere.[4]

Beauvoir's point was precisely that this cannot be done, for the question of the justification for the organization of social reality is a substantive normative question that requires a substantive answer. It is the question of how we *ought* to organize social reality, of which types of organization are justifiable, and which are not. The biological facts are just facts, brute facts, and no matter what those facts are, they do not entail an answer to the normative question. Beauvoir thought that there might even be biological inequality between the sexes (males are larger, women menstruate, etc.), but from that nothing should follow about gender inequality. If anything, social organization should make up for biological inequality.

What is Butler's complaint about the Beauvoirean account? First, she points out that feminist scholars have argued that the notion of *nature* and the relation between *nature* and *culture*, which is presupposed by the Beauvoirean account, are quite problematic. The account assumes that nature is something passive, acted upon (and controlled) by culture, and does not take into account that, as Butler puts it, "[the concept of] nature has a history, and not merely a social one, but, also, that sex is positioned ambiguously in relation to that concept and its history" (1993: 5).

How are we to understand the complaint that the Beauvoirean account misses that the concept of nature has a history? I think that we have to assume that her complaint is that it is not only what is social that is constructed, but that what is natural isn't so untainted as the Beauvoirean assumed. But why should that follow from the fact that the concept of nature has a history?

To say that the concept of nature has a history seems to me to mean any or all of the following:

1. that over time what has counted as natural has changed, that is, the extension of the concept *natural* has undergone change;
2. that over time the content of the concept has changed, that is, the constitutive criteria for being natural have changed;[5]
3. that over time people's beliefs about what is natural have changed, that is, people's associations with the concept *natural* have changed.

---

[4] I take the social sphere here to have political, economic, legal, cultural, and religious dimensions.
[5] This might raise a worry about on what grounds we consider this the same concept, but let us leave that aside for now.

How would a commitment to any of the above invite one to say that sexual distinctions were constructed? One line of thought might be that if the criterion for being male or female has undergone change, then it follows that what it is to be male or to be female has changed. And if so, how can the male/female distinction help but be constructed? For the assumption is that if the distinction between the sexes is a natural distinction, then it is not changeable.[6]

But such an argument won't do, because the Beauvoirean has an easy response. She will say that the criterion for being male or female is merely an *epistemic* criterion, a way of telling, not a *metaphysical* criterion constitutive of what it is to be male or female. Our conceptions of, or beliefs about, the natural world are, of course, imperfect, and the many proposed criteria for being male or female belong to those. Butler's opponent may think there is a real,[7] natural distinction between male and female, but that our criteria have not yet captured that distinction—have not yet managed to carve nature at its joints. Or she may think that nature has too many joints related to sexual differences and that it is up to us to find criteria to latch on to those joints that are of interest to us.[8]

Either way she goes, it is clear that Butler does not succeed in pointing out a weakness of the Beauvoirean position simply by pointing out that the concept of nature has a history. Something more is needed. What more is in the offing? A quote from *Gender Trouble* (1990: 7) gives us a glimpse of what that is:

> It would make no sense, then, to define gender as the cultural interpretation of sex, if sex itself is a gendered category. Gender ought not to be conceived merely as the cultural inscription of meaning on a pregiven sex (a juridical conception); gender must also designate the very apparatus of production whereby the sexes themselves are established. As a result, gender is not to culture as sex is to nature; gender is also the discursive/cultural means by which "sexed nature" or "a natural sex" is produced and established as "prediscursive," prior to culture, a politically neutral surface on which culture acts. . . . How, then, does gender need to be reformulated to encompass

---

[6] Modulo evolutionary changes, taking place over a long, long time.

[7] I.e., independent of our thought and practices.

[8] One might think that this is a weak kind of constructivism, but the key point is that the proponent of this view is committed to there actually being some joints of nature. Butler is not committed to that. Nor does she seem to deny that, perhaps because she thinks that making claims about how the world is independent of us is not justified, because it is beyond the bounds of sense.

the power relations that produce the effect of a prediscursive sex and so conceal that very operation of discursive production?

We are not yet in a position to evaluate the crucial claim that sex itself is a gendered category, pretending, so to speak, to be one uncontaminated by gender or another value. And we won't be in a position to evaluate this claim until we have gotten to know more about Butler's motivations for her view and the reorientation she is suggesting.

So let us consider one possible motivation. One way to distinguish between constructivism (Butlerian or a more radical kind) and a Beauvoirean view is to say that they disagree about where questions of value arise. The constructivist thinks that questions of value go all the way down, that there isn't a base layer, a layer of fact, at which no questions of value arise. Beauvoir can be seen to be committed to such a base layer of biological, natural facts. What do I mean by "questions of value"? I don't mean merely questions about right and wrong, or what individuals or communities should do; I mean value more broadly, including cognitive value. A main motivation for a constructivist account is the deep-seated belief that questions of value arise in more places than we are aware of. The constructivist is thus often involved in a debunking effort: to show that certain claims to objectivity are unfounded and that any social organization based on such claims is thus unjustified.

The above suggestions are all rather general. What we need to know here is if Butler is indeed motivated by the belief that questions of value go all the way down, then how does that belief get translated into her theoretical proposal? How and where does she locate value, to which the Beauvoirean has been oblivious? My suggestion is that Butler's claim is that certain speech acts that appear to be assertions, which the Beauvoirean holds to be assertions of fact, are speech acts of a different kind. Which speech acts? These contested speech acts include apparent assertions to the effect that someone is of a certain sex and other apparent assertions to the effect that someone belongs to a certain human kind, for example, that Jodie Foster is a woman, that Jamie Lee Curtis is female. It is clear, however, that these are not assertions on Butler's view, but rather Austinean exercitives, where the person in question is assigned a certain role to play, with accompanying norms. Butler disagrees with Austin (1993b: 225) that the people performing an exercitive, such as marrying someone, need themselves have the *authority* to do so, but rather thinks that the power of the exercitive act lies in the performers *citing* the law. In fact, Butler thinks that it is the invocation of convention by citing the law that enables the performer to marry the couple.[9] Not all performers of exercitives need to cite laws or other institutional phenomena, on Butler's view. She thinks that certain speech acts can "accumulate the force of authority" (1993: 227) for performers through the repetition or citation of a prior, authoritative set of practices. The suggestion then is that saying things such as "Jamie Lee Curtis is female" is not to describe an objective, value-free fact, but to assign Curtis a normative role to play.[10]

The claim that questions of value go all the way down might make one think that Butler's position is a radical linguistic constructivist one: everything is constructed, everything is language, or everything is text. This is not Butler's position. In fact, she is eager to distance herself from such a view. Let us examine her arguments against radical linguistic constructivism.

3.4 Butler Distinguished from a Radical Linguistic Constructivist

The problem Butler points to is a two-horned dilemma for the radical linguistic constructivist who attempts to make sense of the Beauvoirean truism that gender is the social significance of sex: either the radical linguistic constructivist shows the limits of her own position, or her view is reduced to linguistic monism (1993: 5). The radical linguistic constructivist is committed to the view that everything is language, text, or discourse. Let us examine the two horns. On both horns, gender is constructed. The problem is what to do about sex.

If the radical linguistic constructivist says that sex itself is unconstructed, then she has conceded that not everything is constructed. Is she then, after all, committed to a view according to which there are things in the world that are not constructed, something like a base layer of natural facts? But if so, then it is hard to see how she differs from the Beauvoirean (except, of course, that her claims appear more inflammatory).

---

[9] Butler 1993: 225: "Indeed, it is through the invocation of convention that the speech act of the judge derives its binding power; that binding power is to be found neither in the subject of the judge nor his will, but in the citational legacy by which a contemporary 'act' emerges in the context of a chain of binding conventions."

[10] I take exercitives to be more apt than verdictives as the category Butler has in mind, as she clearly does not think that the performer of the speech act is attempting to track any independent fact, as verdictives require.

On the other hand, if the radical linguistic constructivist says that sex is itself a linguistic construction, then she is in no better position than the radical linguistic constructivist who rejects the sex/gender distinction altogether. For both, the view is reduced to linguistic monism. That is the unhappy view that everything there is a linguistic construction. For a feminist, the challenge for linguistic monism is particularly acute: How to make sense of material violence against women, of rape, of economic hardship?[11]

Such violence surely is not a linguistic construction, and the very suggestion that it might be is offensive. For if it were a linguistic construction, would it not follow that by changing our language or our discourses we could stop such violence? The very suggestion seems, on the face of it, even contrary to feminist aims. For what would have been the point of the consciousness-raising and the overcoming of our false consciousness, in the beginning of the century for the proletariat, in the seventies for Western women? Did we create social problems by beginning to be able to describe aspects of the world in a different way? Certainly not. Isn't there an important sense in which there was already something harmful happening, and the availability of the description made us able to recognize it? This is an additional problem for the linguistic constructivist who got caught in the other horn. However, whereas that horn exposed an internal problem to the position, this one (merely) poses an external problem. It is of course a stronger criticism to be able not only to point out that a view doesn't do what one thinks it should aim to do, but also to show that the view cannot do what its proponents intend it to do.

In light of the difficulties that a feminist radical linguistic constructivist faces, it is not surprising that many feminists have thought that feminism needs to assume that sex is unconstructed just like the Beauvoireans do. Butler thinks that it is misguided to think that a feminist theory cannot proceed without presuming the materiality of women's bodies, or, in her phrase, the *materiality of sex* (1992: 17). The radical linguistic constructivist position is, to be sure, problematic, as it seems unable to make sense of the material violence women suffer. Butler thinks, however, that the options are not exhausted by *presuming* materiality or *negating* it (1992: 17). What is needed is a rethinking of the sex/gender distinction, but perhaps more importantly, a complete shift in orientation—something of a Kantian "Copernican Revolution."

---

[11] See also Butler 1992: 17.

3.5 The Elements of Butler's View

For Butler, then, the question is no longer "How is gender constituted as and through a certain interpretation of sex? (a question that leaves matter untheorized), BUT: through what regulatory norms is sex itself materialized?" (1993: 10).

If sexual categories are not joints of nature, what are they then, and why did we ever think they were joints of nature? Butler's suggestion is that sexual categories are *regulatory ideals* (1993: 1). This term is borrowed from Foucault, but has its roots in Kant. What is a regulatory ideal? It is a prescriptive norm projected or posited by subjects, as opposed to, say, read off of nature, so to speak. An ideally rational agent is such a norm, for instance: it is an ideal because no actual person is an ideally rational agent, and it is regulatory because there is a demand on all of us that we strive to be such (although we never will be). Butler's suggestion is that the categories of male and female are such ideals,[12] although I believe that she thinks that the demand on us that we strive for one of those ideals is not grounded in the same way as the demand that we strive for rational agency. For part of her aim is a debunking one: to show that this demand on us is a demand to the effect that we help perpetuate the current power structure and that the force of that demand does not come from its being a justified demand, but merely from its being a demand backed with power (1993: 35).[13]

Coupled with the claim that the category of sex is a regulatory ideal comes a story of what is involved in saying that someone is of a certain sex.[14] In the case of the Beauvoireans, saying that S is female amounts to asserting a fact, describing what (a part of) the world is like. Not so for Butler. It is an exercitive act, to use Austinean language. To say that S

---

[12] This is not to say that we can choose which ideal we strive for.

[13] See also Butler 1990: 6–7: "The radical splitting of the gendered subject poses yet another set of problems. Can we refer to a 'given' sex or a 'given' gender without first inquiring into how sex and/or gender is given, through what means? And what is 'sex' anyway? Is it natural, anatomical, chromosomal, or hormonal, and how is a feminist critic to assess the scientific discourses which purport to establish such 'fact' for us? Does sex have a history? Does each sex have a different history, or histories? Is there a history of how the duality of sex was established, a genealogy that might expose the binary options as a variable construction? Are the ostensibly natural facts of sex discursively produced by various scientific discourses in the service of political and social interests [false taxonomies?]? If the immutable character of sex is contested, perhaps this construct called 'sex' is as culturally constructed as gender; indeed, perhaps it was always already gender, with the consequence that the distinction between sex and gender turns out to be no distinction at all."

[14] Butler does not have to say that all utterances analogous to "She is female" or "It's a girl" fall in that category, only that those that are backed by authority (via a successful citation) do.

is female is to assign S a role and to express a commitment—one's own or that of the community—that S be female and be regarded as female (1992: 17).[15] It is an effective act of speech because it cites established gender practices that have normative force in the community, irrespective of the standing of the speaker.

An analogy may be helpful here. Consider a game called the "gender game." The game involves a host of complicated rules for behavior within the game. There are only two types of role a player can play: either one enters the game as a girl or as a boy, and with time one advances to different stages of that role (the man or the woman stage), giving one different duties and responsibilities and different possible moves.

Now, there has been no mention of sex yet. What would be the role of sex in my hypothetical gender game? If my analogy is to work, then there has to be a place for sex within the gender game. I suggest that in the gender game the categories of sex are projected regulatory ideals, ideals that best fit the perpetuation of the game. In fact, they are gendered ideals, that is, shaped by gender rules that regulate what bodies and body parts have meaning within the game. How exactly? I would like to attempt to link it to Butler's idea that "'to matter' means at once 'to materialize' and 'to mean'" (1993: 32). I take this to mean that in this context the bodies that matter in the gender game are those that are materialized in accordance with the rules of the game; they are the intelligible bodies. It is then the matrix of intelligibility—in other words, the rules of the gender game—that governs the materialization of the bodies that come to matter to the game. Let us take Butler's own example (1993: 7):

> Consider the medical interpellation which (the recent emergence of the sonogram notwithstanding) shifts an infant from an "it" to a "she" or a "he," and in that naming, the girl is "girled," brought into the domain of language and kinship through the interpellation of gender. But that

---

[15] Cf. Butler 1990: 17: "the question here will be: To what extent do regulatory practices of gender formation and division constitute identity, the internal coherence of the subject, indeed, the self-identical status of the person? To what extent is 'identity' a normative ideal rather than a descriptive feature of experience? And how do the regulatory practices that govern gender also govern culturally intelligible notions of identity? In other words, the 'coherence' and 'continuity' of 'the person' are not logical or analytical features of personhood, but, rather, socially instituted and maintained norms of intelligibility. Inasmuch as 'identity' is assured through the stabilizing concepts of sex, gender, and sexuality, the very notion of 'the person' is called into question by the cultural emergence of those 'incoherent' or 'discontinuous' gendered beings who appear to be persons but who fail to conform to the gendered norms of cultural intelligibility by which persons are defined."

"girling" of the girl does not end there; on the contrary, that founding interpellation is reiterated by various authorities and throughout various intervals of time to reenforce or contest this naturalized effect. The naming is at once the setting of a boundary, and also the repeated inculcation of a norm.

Before the baby is girled, it is not yet part of the gender game; it does not fit into the scheme of things, is not part of the symbolic domain: it does not yet *matter*. What there is before the naming is unintelligible (in the game), and it is only through being articulated as a girl that the girl comes into being as a participant in the game.[16]

What might the mechanism be, by which sex gets materialized? Here Butler's Foucauldean story has decidedly Hegelian elements. Let me sketch the Hegelian expressivist account of the development of the subject, and of objectification. I then suggest that these two models are the mechanism by which sex gets materialized, gendered, and rendered intelligible, on Butler's story.

The Hegelian expressivist idea is roughly as follows. A subject forms a conception or model of itself and its relation to the world, followed by the acting out or actualization of this conception. To "act out" a conception is, roughly speaking, to behave as if that conception were true and strive to make it apply, make it true, "perform" that identity. How so? With a conception are associated norms for behavior, and to act out a particular conception is to take those norms as binding on oneself and to strive to act in accordance with them.

The other side of the coin is the story of objectification, which goes as follows. The self or subject forms a conception of the object and attempts to actualize that conception. This the self does by acting as if the object conforms to the conception the self has of it. This is thus a third-party identification, followed by an attempt to make that identification apply. The objectification succeeds if the object does not, or is not able to, resist the conception offered of it by the subject. In perhaps the most interesting case, the object is itself a subject, a self. In that case, it may react to the objectification in either of two ways: (1) take on the conception imposed on it and attempt to actualize that conception; or (2) fight the

---

[16] Cf. Butler 1990: 8: "Bodies cannot be said to have a signifiable existence prior to the mark of their gender; the question then emerges: To what extent does the body come into being in and through the mark(s) of gender? How do we reconceive the body no longer as a passive medium or instrument awaiting the enlivening capacity of a distinctly immaterial will?"

objectification and the conception imposed and attempt to (re)claim control over its self-conception.

Let me draw these elements together a bit more and address how they work together in a social setting. Let's think about these *conceptions* a subject may adopt as a conception of itself. In a particular social or cultural context, there are several such conceptions that may be available to a subject to adopt as its own, but, importantly, the subject's choice is constrained by the available conceptions. We can think of them as conceptions of what it is to be a member of some social category and the associated norms of behavior for members of that category. Only conceptions that appear to fit us "well enough" are available for our adoption, and often certain socially salient conceptions are thrust upon us and we must negotiate other people's acting as if that were our conception. For instance, the conception of what it is to be a woman is not only available to me but thrust upon me every day, and I embrace it more or less and act out that conception every day: I act as if it were true, and the more I act as if it were true, the more accurately it fits me. This is so, even if I negotiate what comes with adopting that conception to some extent. Some of the norms of behavior associated with being a woman I embrace fully and take as binding on me; others I try to resist. Sometimes this resistance is without any repercussions; sometimes it results in social sanctions of some kind.

The two components of the Hegelian model work together to form the subjects within the gender game and to perpetuate the gender game itself. The first experience a player in the gender game has of the game is of being handed a conception that he or she is to act out. She or he is, in a sense, treated as an object. Then, the better the player acts out the conception offered, the better she or he does in the game. The objectification has likewise worked to the same degree, since she or he has taken over the conception offered and started to act out that conception.

How does the discussion of the two parts of the Hegelian model help us understand the process of materialization of sex within the gender game? Let us think about which bodies and body parts come to have meaning within the game. They are the bodies and body parts that do not resist the conceptions imposed on them. The available conceptions are all ones that fit the perpetuation of the gender game itself. What sex is, is whatever conforms to the gendered ideals. The subjects' conceptions of themselves as embodied beings, and the conceptions of their own bodies and the significance of each body part, even what counts as a body part, are all shaped by the gender rules, the matrix of gender. And it is even part of the gender game that sex be thought of as not contaminated by the gendering, but as a natural category. Such naturalization of sex is a necessary part of the perpetuation of the gender game itself.[17] How so? Treating sex distinctions as natural makes them seem inevitable and as the source of gender distinctions and hierarchies in a way that legitimates them and thereby the gender game itself. Naturalizing sex is thus a big part of the ideology that helps perpetuate the gender game.

3.6 Butler's Proposal: Life Is a Gender Game

I take it that Butler's proposal is that a game like the gender game is what we live in.[18] I now want to explore the significance of that claim for the question of what kind of metaphysics Butler is offering.

For one thing, Butler has suggested a reorientation: our assertions do not fit the world, but the world fits our assertions. It is the Kantian suggestion that we shape our world more than we have hitherto realized. But the Kantian inheritance does not end with that. For the structure of the domain of the gender game and its relation to what is outside the game can be explained by an analogy to Kant's transcendental idealism.

The analogy works as follows: the realm of the gender game is like Kant's phenomenal realm. It is the realm of spatiotemporality (materiality) and intelligibility. There is another realm, but what resides there can only be thought,[19] but the thought about those objects is not contentful. For Kant, the phenomenal realm is the realm of objects as they are for us, as they are subject to the conditions of possible experience. The noumenal realm, on the other hand, is the realm of objects as they are independent of those conditions. The Butlerian symbolic domain is the domain of signifiability and intelligibility (1993: 138). The objects we

---

[17] Cf. Butler 1990: 33: "To expose the contingent acts that create the appearance of a naturalistic necessity, a move which has been part of cultural critique at least since Marx, is a task that now takes on the added burden of showing how the very notion of the subject, intelligible only through its appearance as gendered, admits of possibilities that have been forcibly foreclosed by the various reifications of gender that have constituted its contingent ontologies."

[18] Cf. Butler 1990: 16: "It would be wrong to think that the discussion of 'identity' ought to proceed prior to a discussion of gender identity for the simple reason that 'persons' only become intelligible through becoming gendered in conformity with recognizable standards of gender intelligibility."

[19] Cf. Butler 1993: 8: "Paradoxically, the inquiry into the kinds of erasures and exclusions by which the construction of the subject operates is no longer constructivism, but neither is it essentialism. For there is an 'outside' to what is constructed by discourse, but this is not an absolute 'outside,' an ontological thereness that exceeds or counters the boundaries of discourse; as a constitutive 'outside,' it is that which can only be thought—when it can—in relation to that discourse, at and as its most tenuous borders."

experience there are objects as they are subject to the conditions of the gender game, the gender matrix. We can think of objects as they are independent of those conditions, but in certain cases such thoughts will not be very contentful, because gender influences the way such objects appear to us so completely. The suggestion is that sex is such an object, and that we cannot think about sex or sexualized objects contentfully or experience them independent of the conditions of gender. But does this mean that we are stuck with the current gendering of sex? Not at all. I think Butler might say that although we may not be able to think or experience sex independently of the conditions of gender, the actual conditions of gender need not be the conditions that sex is subject to. But then what is needed for change is, in the first instance, a critical examination of our actual gender norms.

The Kantian analogy breaks down when one points to objects that can contentfully be thought about or experienced as not subject to the conditions of the gender game. But that is alright. Butler can allow that the gender game is not the only game in town,[20] and that in fact it interacts with other games, some of which can be just as oppressive as the gender game. However, I think the Kantian analogy helps us to situate Butler's position in the ontological landscape in between the Beauvoirean and the radical linguistic constructivist. Let us recall what the relationship is between sex and gender on Butler's story. Instead of sex being a natural category, and gender the social significance of sex, sex is really a gendered category posited by us and claimed to be a natural one so that it can better help perpetuate the gender game. Gender categories, on the other hand, are roles or ideals constitutive of the gender game itself. How does Butler's ontological picture then compare to the Beauvoirean one? Contrary to the Beauvoirean, she thinks that all sex is constructed or materialized through the matrix of gender. After her shift in orientation, Butler's point that the concept of nature has a history appears stronger, since she is able to resist the Beauvoirean move that the criteria we are talking about are purely epistemic ones. Butler will insist that the criteria for sex distinctions are indeed constitutive criteria of what it is to be male or female. However, the significance of being male or female is tied up with what meaning it has within the gender game.

Although sex is constructed on Butler's view, her position does not collapse into linguistic monism with the radical linguistic constructivist. For she is not interested in the claim that there isn't anything before the

---

[20] For example, the race game, the class game, the ethnic game.

materialization in accordance with the matrix of gender. The point is rather that whatever meaning and significance sex and sexualized body parts have, they have in virtue of being given to us as gendered, for it is the gender matrix that is the matrix of intelligibility for sexed objects.

3.7 Critique

My interpretation of Butler's constructivism has centered around four ideas. Let me tie them more closely together. Firstly, I suggested that Butler is not merely advocating a rethinking of the sex/gender distinction, but a complete shift in orientation. This is a Kantian "Copernican Revolution" of sorts: the picture is not that our thought and practices conform to how the world is, but that, at least sometimes, the world conforms to our thought and practices. I appealed to a rethinking of what is going on when it is claimed that someone is of a certain sex, and I suggested that instead of thinking of that apparent assertion as a mere assertion of fact—of how the world is—that we think of it as an assignment of a normative role, through an exercitive act. The suggestion then is that apparent assertions that someone is of a certain sex, that some body parts and acts are sexualized, are such assignments of roles, and that our thought and practices partake in making them true through our exercitive acts. I then appealed to the analogy with a gender game to explain how bodies and body parts acquire meaning within our thought and practices. Such an acquisition of meaning goes hand in hand with the materialization of the body and body parts within the game. The actual mechanism of materialization I then tried to explain by reference to Hegel's expressivist model of the development of the subject and his model of objectification. Finally, I attempted to explain the relationship between the conditions of intelligibility within the gender game, and that which is outside the game by reference to Kant's distinction between the phenomenal and the noumenal realms. That analogy is also supposed to help us see how Butler's ontology differs from the Beauvoirean one and that of the radical linguistic constructivist.

If Butler is right, and it is not only that the category of sex is gendered, but that the naturalization of it is a necessary part of the perpetuation of the gender hierarchy, then not only can she resist the Beauvoirean position, but she also poses a positive challenge to the Beauvoirean feminist (1990: 5):

> Is the construction of the category of female as a coherent and stable subject an unwitting regulation and reification of gender relations? And is not

such a reification precisely contrary to feminist aims? To what extent does the category of female achieve stability and coherence only in the context of the gendered matrix?

I'm inclined to think that the critique Butler offers of the Beauvoirean position is right on target and the claim that sex gets materialized in accordance with the matrix of gender is both illuminating and accurate. The worry I have is what happens to the biologically given on this picture: out of what does sex get materialized? Why are some people better able to pass as male or female than other people? Doesn't that have something to do with certain biological features that are simply given and that no amount of interpretation can make disappear? Isn't it the case that only people with certain functioning body parts can bear offspring with people with certain other functioning body parts? Butler's account does not seem to be able to explain that. In fact, her account seems open to the charge that in principle any body part could be a sexed body part and that there is no biological (as opposed to social) reason why some body parts have sexual significance and not others. I think we need an account of the construction of sex that takes seriously the gendered societal influences on that process, but that also gives the constraints of nature their due.

I think that saying that someone is woman is an act of *placing*,[21] and not a simple Austinean exercitive, and thus has both a verdictive and exercitive component, whereas on my reading, Butler takes it as only having an excercitive dimension, because there is no independent fact that people are attempting to track.

3.8 Conclusion

In this chapter, I have drawn up a picture of the two prominent ways to account for the metaphysics of gender and sex categories: the Beauvoirean one and Judith Butler's. On the Beauvoirean view, sex is biologically given and gender is the social significance of sex, and on Butler's account, sex is a regulative ideal that is posited to ground demands for people's adherence to society's gender schemas. The account that I propose in the next chapter owes a lot to both theorists, but diverges from both in how to

---

[21] And saying that someone is female can be a classifying act, when done by an authority. It can also in certain contexts be an assertion attempting to track how the individual is classified, or attempting to track the presence of body parts. Also, sometimes it is a placing in a gender category (even though the word "female" is used).

deal with "nature" and the "natural." As we saw, the post-Beauvoirean was happy to allow that sex was a natural phenomenon, where nature and the natural were untainted by culture or social practices. This was, in fact, the starting point in Butler's reorientation. Butler, on the other hand, makes no room for anything that is uncontaminated by culture or social or conceptual practices. The conferralist framework that I have offered allows me to accept Butler's reorientation and the view that culture and social practices contaminate what we take to be natural more than we think without doing away with constraints on our social world imposed by nature. Let us now turn to the application of that framework and the associated conception of social construction to the case of sex and gender and then to some of the other "usual suspects": race, disability, sexual orientation, and religion.

CHAPTER 4 | Conferralism about Sex and Gender

HOW CAN WE do justice to Butler's insight that sex is materialized through the lens of gender, without denying that there are any constraints on nature's part in what gets sexed? I suggest the conferralist framework and the conception of social construction I have articulated are particularly well equipped to accommodate that insight, while allowing for a distinction between sex and gender, and in that way, accommodating a key Beauvoirean insight.

4.1 Conferralism about Sex

The conferralist paradigm can help us make sense of the value-ladenness of a property or category, without denying that there is anything prior to the conferral, as I interpret Butler to be committed to. It can thus help us make sense of the appearance that a certain property is biologically given, even if it is not. Sex, I believe, is such a property. Being of a certain sex is a conferred property. In fact, it is an institutional property.

What are my reasons for thinking that sex is not a biological property but an institutional one? This is the thought: if a property chiefly figures in explanations of social facts, and not natural facts, that suggests that the property is a social property, and not a natural property. Consider, for example, the natural facts about what kind of human bodies can create offspring together. It is not your sex assignment that allows you to bear or seed children.[1] In fact, people whose sex assignment is in no way in dispute

---

[1] I count both the egg and the sperm as "seeds" here, contra the Aristotelian conception of the contribution of the woman as that of the fertile soil for the man's seed. Thanks to Laurie Shrage for this point.

cannot bear or seed children. What allows one to bear or seed children is rather some other properties that the sex assignment is intended to track. Since being of a certain sex is not an explanatory property when it comes to the bearing or seeding of offspring, but it is explanatory when it comes to the distribution of various social resources, privileges, and burdens, doesn't that suggest that sex is a social property and not a natural one?[2]

Here is thus my methodological suggestion: one should consider in what kinds of explanations the property occurs. If it functions in explanations of various social facts and it isn't playing the explanatory role of various physical or natural facts, but rather some "nearby" property is doing so, that should give us reason to think that the property in question is a social property, and hence conferred.

The second step in offering a conferral account of a property such as being of a certain sex is to tell a plausible story of how the mechanisms of conferral actually work. This is where social metaphysics has to rely on the empirical to offer a plausible story of the nature of the social phenomenon in question. In my story of the mechanism of conferral, I rely on the work of Anne Fausto-Sterling and others and, again, Judith Butler.

A host of recent work in biology by Anne Fausto-Sterling and others reveals that the biology supposedly supporting the division into two sexes is quite messy (Fausto-Sterling 2000a, 2000b; Roughgarden 2004; Callahan 2009). If we look at three main ways of dividing people into sexes (by functioning genitalia, chromosomes, and hormonal levels), not only do these three methods not divide people into two neat groups, female and male, but the hard cases do not line up: someone may not fit neatly into one of the categories according to one method, yet do so according to the others. The three ways of dividing people up into sexes not only do not carve nature at some joint where you have female on one side and male on the other; these three methods of carving carve up different slices of nature.

But "carving" is not only to be used metaphorically in this context. Even before voluntary sex change operations, newborns with ambiguous sex characteristics have been subject to the scalpel (2000b). Fausto-Sterling estimates that somewhere around 1.7 percent of people are intersex according to one or other of the methods used.

---

[2] This is consistent with the idea that some notion of sex could be useful as an explanatory category in biology, e.g., as an imperfect shorthand for some other features and thus making use of a sex distinction could have some predictive value, even if it is a false taxonomy, to use Gould's term (2000).

For these reasons, I want to give an account of the property of being of a certain sex as a conferred property where the aim is to track certain physical features, but where the resulting property is an institutional property, in fact a legal one:[3]

Property: being female, male[4]

Who: legal authorities, drawing on the expert opinion of doctors, other medical personnel, and parents

What: the recording of a sex in official documents, on the basis of the testimony of parents, doctors, and others. The judgment of the doctors (and others) as to what sex role might be most fitting, given the biological characteristics present

When: at birth (in the case of newborns); after surgery and hormonal treatment (in the case of older individuals)

Base property: the aim is to track as many sex-stereotypical characteristics as possible, and doctors perform surgery in cases where that might help bring the physical characteristics more in line with the stereotype of male and female

In giving this account of how sex gets conferred, I draw on Butler's work, as interpreted in the last chapter, as well as Fausto-Sterling's work. The Butlerian elements should be clear: Sex assignment is guided by the aim to have the individual in question exhibit as many sex-stereotypical properties as possible, with the aid of medical treatment, if necessary. It isn't quite that the gender matrix dictates the materialization of sex, as Butler would have it, but that sex stereotypes, shaped by societal expectations about gender roles and possible ways of being within a society, guide sex assignment. On this account, it isn't the case, as on Butler's, that there are no natural constraints on the materialization of sex, as determined by the gender matrix, for people have various physical properties. But the determination of which physical properties are important for sex assignment, and, in particular, the assignment of people into one of two sexes, is shaped by societal values and interests. And by making biological properties be what the conferrers are attempting to track, we can account for the appearance that sex is biologically given, even if it is not.

---

[3] There can be other institutional properties labeled "sex" operating in other contexts, for example medical contexts, with different base properties.

[4] There are jurisdictions in which it is possible to be a third sex, for example, Australia.

While the above account of sex accurately reflects the sex categories in most Western countries and many others in the beginning of the twenty-first century, there may come a time when sex-status options are more numerous or when sex status need not be specified.

What we have here is an account of sex that can be part of a debunking project: it may appear that the category in question is a natural one, but in fact it is a conferred legal status. The conferral framework can help expose sex for what it is; it also gives us a diagnosis of why it appears to be a natural category. But we can do even better. When we consider the explanatory function of a sex assignment, a general method for constructing an argument for the social construction of a certain kind suggests itself: Consider what kinds of facts the presence of the property explains. If it only explains social facts, is it not likely that it is a social property and hence conferred?

4.2 Conferralism about Gender

As the discussion so far has made clear, I aim to capture the type of social construction involved in the post-Beauvoirean feminist slogan: gender is the social significance of sex. But there is a twist. In fact there are two: sex is not biologically given, and gender is radically context dependent.

Consider this scenario: you work as a coder in San Francisco. You go into your office where you are one of the guys. After work, you tag along with some friends at work to a bar. It is a very heteronormative space, and you are neither a guy nor a gal. You are an other. You walk up the street to another bar where you are a butch and expected to buy drinks for the femmes. Then you head home to your grandmother's eightieth birthday party, where you help out in the kitchen with the other women while the men smoke cigars.[5]

---

[5] It is easy to think of anecdotes that fit the various context descriptions. My friend, Agustín Rayo, told me a nice story of going with his mother, Julieta Fierro, a famous astronomer and public figure, to a genderly rigid gathering of extended family in Mexico. Apparently the expectations were that the women would get together early in the morning on Sundays to start cooking the meal, and the men would gather and drink beer and tequila and chat over the soccer on television. Later the men would be seated at the table and the women would wait on them while they ate. Only after the men were done eating would the women eat the leftovers. While Agustín's mother was a bad fit in each company, she ended up sitting and eating with the men. There was never a repeat of that family experiment. The way I analyze this example is that it is not that Julieta Fierro counted as a woman or a man in that context. This was precisely the kind of context where there was no gender available to her. She was treated as an other. While she ended up conversing and eating with the men, the fact that she ceased to partake in such family gatherings suggests that the categories

In each of the contexts in which we travel, different features of ourselves are socially salient. That is also true of gender contexts. In some contexts, people are trying to track a sex assignment, in others a role in societal organization, a bodily presentation, a role in the preparation of food, a role in biological reproduction, a role as a sexual partner, and so on.

In many gender contexts, there may be a persistent assumption in the background that in tracking one of the base properties—that is, sex assignment, role in biological reproduction, sexual role, role in societal organization, and so on—we manage to track the other phenomena as well. But even if there are many contexts where this assumption is not misplaced, the presence of the many contexts where it is an erroneous assumption shows the importance of keeping these various base properties apart, not only for a better theoretical understanding, but for practical reasons. In fact, a variety of feminist and queer theoretical work and activism has been aimed at challenging this assumption: these categories are not coextensive, and tracking one of these properties need not help us track the others.[6]

It is for this reason that my own suggestion as to how gender is conferred makes gender be highly context dependent, and the base property or properties vary with context. On this view, not only is gender deeply context dependent when it comes to historical periods and geographical locations, but the same geographical location and time period can allow for radically different contexts, so that a person may count as of a certain gender in some contexts and not others. This is because different properties are being tracked in different contexts: in some contexts, it is the person's perceived role in biological reproduction, in others it is the role in societal organization of various kinds, sexual engagement, bodily presentation, preparation of food at family gatherings, and so on. Here is the general schema:

Conferred property: being of gender G, for example, a woman, man, trans*
Who: the subjects with standing in the particular context

---

available to her were not comfortable and there was not a comfortable "third gender" category available in the context.

[6] This is why in some contexts lesbians don't quite count as women, and that in some contexts butch lesbians are more challenging than femmes, as they very obviously trouble the assumption that all of the gender-stereotypical properties inhere in the same person.

What: the perception of the subject S that the person has the base property P

When: in some particular context

Base property: the base property P, for example, the role in biological reproduction; in others it is the person's role in societal organization of various kinds, sexual engagement, bodily presentation, preparation of food at family gatherings, self-identification, and so on

Gender is a communal property and is conferred in each and every context we find ourselves in. In that, I agree with Butler, as I interpret her in the last chapter, and Charlotte Witt (2011): there is no escaping gender. As Witt puts it (2011:92), gender is a megasocial role that inflects all other social roles we find ourselves in. And for Butler, we are born into a gender game and only exit the game when we exit for good.

Let's linger on how gender gets conferred in a particular context. Consider a party. Gender gets conferred by other partygoers with standing, who cite social arrangements that exist outside the context of the particular party, namely those that have been operating in other contexts in which the partygoers have been. I think of them as gender maps that each person brings to the party. These gender maps come with gender roles that have constraints and enablements attached to them. What gets negotiated at the party is which gender map should operate at the party, who should play what gender role, and what the content of each role should be. What this highly contextualized account of gender brings out is the systematic and structural aspect of gender (by means of the gender maps that have been brought to the context from the other contexts the people have traveled in),[7] yet it reveals how the enforcers of this structure are always individual agents in contexts. The assignment of gender roles in a context draws its force from how broadly and widely the gender maps are operating, even though resistance and negotiation can and do happen in many contexts. But as Witt (2011:32) has argued, individuals are responsive to, and evaluated with respect to, social norms irrespective of their endorsing those norms; this point is crucial. The subjects in the context need not endorse the gender map that is operative in the context in order to be subject to it.

On this view, there may be certain contexts such that to be a certain gender one need not only be perceived to have some base property, such as a specific role in biological reproduction, but also not be seen to trouble

---

[7] More on that in chapter 6.

the assumption that one also has some other properties traditionally associated with that gender (for example, a societal role, gender-appropriate presentation, or sexual orientation). There can thus be contexts where there may be people who do not count as being of any of the available genders. Similarly, being transgender will count as one of only two genders in some contexts, while as a separate gender in some other contexts; in yet others, it will raise trouble for the gendering structure of that context and disrupt the expectations of the coextension of the associated base properties. In certain contexts, being perceived as being of a certain sex may be an essential base property; in other contexts, it may be highly irrelevant. And increasingly, there are contexts in which self-identification is what people are attempting to track: if you are taken to identify with being a woman in a context, you are a woman in that context.

Let us now turn to the question how an account like the one presented here is a social constructionist account of gender. On this account, a (base) feature of a person is socially significant in a context such that people taken to have that feature get conferred onto them a social status in the context. The social status is the socially constructed feature.

What is the role of the recipients of the conferred status? What if they don't want to be of the gender they are assigned? There are several things that may happen in a particular context: persons can resist the conferral of the property (the gender assignment), but it will vary how successful such resistance can be. Certain contexts may be particularly "silencing" in this regard, such that attempts to trouble one's gender assignment receive no uptake and remain futile. This is analogous to what can happen in linguistic contexts where it can be impossible to say certain things. Try as one may, the context may prevent one from being heard and understood as saying what one intends to say.[8]

Similarly, one may try to trouble people's perception of oneself in a particular context, but there may be no other gender assignment available. Some contexts are even such that there is no possibility of simply not fitting into one of the available genders. Just as in some linguistic contexts it may be impossible to say what one wants to say, so there can be some action contexts where it is impossible to perform the actions one wants to perform, because the performance of the action depends on one's being taken to perform it (or less strictly, taken to have certain features).

---

[8] Consider, e.g., being an actor on stage and attempting to warn a theater audience that there is a fire in the theater by shouting "fire!" where the audience continues to laugh (Maitra 2004, 2009).

On this account of gender, there is thus no one context-independent property of being of a certain gender, for example, a woman. Instead, what we have is a family of context-dependent conferred properties, some of which share some base properties.

4.3 The North Carolina Bathroom Bill and the Sex/Gender Distinction

In 2016, the North Carolina state legislature passed a law that, among other things, required people to use bathrooms that corresponded to the sex on their birth certificates (HB2).[9] This means, among other things, that people who identify as women may not use the women's bathroom unless their birth certificate says that they are female. Does this case trouble the idea that there is a sex/gender distinction? Does it trouble my accounts of sex and gender and their relationship?

I don't think so. I think, on the contrary, that the conferralist framework has the flexibility and nuance to deal with that sort of case and that this case shows off some of its strengths particularly well.

I think of this case as one where the state legislature has created new *institutional gender* categories,[10] for the purposes of bathroom use in North Carolina, where the base property for the conferral is the sex assignment on the birth certificate. As a result of passing the law, persons are only *entitled* to use the women's bathroom if their sex assignment on their birth certificate is female. This is true for those people whose birth certificate was issued shortly after birth and also for those whose certificate was issued after sex reassignment surgery and hormonal treatment. Then the question is how this law gets enforced. Do the police sit outside bathrooms asking people for their birth certificates before they enter the stalls? Certainly not. Bathroom use is policed by other users. But no one asks anyone for birth certificates. Instead, people eye each other, and depending on your presumed sex assignment, you are given the communal status woman and allowed to use the stall without harassment or not. Physical characteristics such as sex-stereotypical body hair and

---

[9] The official name is An Act to Provide for Single-Sex Multiple Occupancy Bathroom and Changing Facilities in Schools and Public Agencies and to Create Statewide Consistency in Regulation of Employment and Public Accommodations, Session Law 2016-3, House Bill 2. Available at http://www.ncleg.net/Sessions/2015E2/Bills/House/PDF/H2v4.pdf.

[10] These are distinct from the already-existing sex categories.

gender-typical physical build[11] are used as evidence for what your sex assignment might be.

But here is the complication in the North Carolina case. According to the law, you are entitled to use the women's bathroom if your sex assignment on your birth certificate is female, but people in bathrooms are not attempting to track your birth certificate sex assignment. If you have had sex reassignment surgery and your new birth certificate says you are female, you still will be accosted in most bathroom situations where people support the HB2 legislation, even if you are legally entitled to use the bathroom. That shows that the bathroom spaces are in fact communal spaces where the base property is a different one from the one specified by the legislation. Perhaps the base properties are a cluster of features including stereotypical secondary sex characteristics as well as body language and presentation; if the gender presentation doesn't line up with the sex presentation, there can be trouble.

If we think of it like this, then we characterize the political struggle going on in North Carolina in 2017 as a struggle over which properties should be the base properties in the conferral of gender in the context of bathrooms. The North Carolina legislature insists that sex assignment on the current birth certificate should be the base property, and the community policing in certain bathroom contexts, where gender presentation and sex presentation need to line up with presumed sex on the original birth certificate, is even more severe. Activism led by LGBTQ people and their allies is focused on the claim that self-identification should be the base property for the conferral of gender for the purposes of bathroom use.

Other bathroom contexts may function differently. When I landed at the Ataturk airport in Istanbul in 2012, I went to the women's bathroom along with many of my fellow travelers from the plane from Berlin. This included a tall, muscular woman, who showed no indication of having ambiguous or conflicting sex-stereotypical characteristics, but she wore jeans, a jacket, and no makeup. As we entered the bathroom, she was shouted at and harassed by the other women in the room. They did not want her in the bathroom, not because of her sex assignment, but because of her gender presentation. I have my doubts that had she gone into the men's bathroom, she would have received a warmer welcome. I interpret this situation such

---

[11] The statistical difference in size and build between men and women is only partly due to biological factors, including chromosomes, but also due to difference in gender norms regarding physical exercise, physical work, muscle build, and the like. The physical differences then increase over time.

that the base properties for the gender conferral in this context wasn't sex assignment, but rather self-presentation in accordance with gender norms regarding posture, body language, clothing, and such.

There are battles going on over gender right now, perhaps like never before. The struggles for liberation from the confines of our many gender contexts are led by people who flout gender norms and those who refuse to be confined to the sex they were assigned at birth and the oft-associated gender that comes with it.

4.4 Comparison with Other Accounts of Gender

We have seen how the accounts of gender and sex offered here differ from the Beauvoirean one and from Butler's. Let me now discuss how it differs from other recent accounts that take gender to be a social position, social role, or social status, those of Sally Haslanger, Linda Alcoff, and Charlotte Witt. I then compare the account to that of Talia Bettcher, whose account of gender attribution involves context-dependency. I have learned a tremendous amount from all of them and will not give detailed criticisms of their views here, but rather focus on the main differences between their accounts and mine.[12]

4.4.1 Sally Haslanger

We saw that Haslanger's account does justice to the post-Beauvoirean feminist slogan, *gender is the social significance of sex*, and that gender is constructed through people taken to have features indicative of a role in biological reproduction. At a first glance, it may appear that the main differences between my account and Haslanger's are that she builds hierarchy into her account of gender and that she privileges the perceived role in biological reproduction as the feature that determines a person's status, while on my account, base properties vary and gender is radically context dependent. But these differences betray a deeper difference in methodology. Haslanger's account of gender is a class analysis, with a twist. If hers were a class analysis of gender following a simple materialist formula, then genders would be social classes defined by their relation to the means of reproduction, and in that inherently relational. But Haslanger's

---

[12] There are other recent accounts of gender that I won't discuss here, as they are sufficiently different from mine, so they are unlikely to be confused with mine. These include Stoljar 1995, 2011; Bach 2012; McKitrick 2015; Jenkins 2015.

account is both materialist and post-Beauvoirean: gender is the social significance of sex. How are we to reconcile these two commitments?

Perhaps we can do so like this: Perhaps sex also demands a class analysis. Perhaps sexes are to be defined in terms of their actual relation to the means of reproduction. Then a gender is the social significance of a particular position in that relational structure. And persons are of a particular gender if they are taken to stand in a certain relation to the means of reproduction.

If this were Haslanger's view, there would be some problems in hard cases.[13] Consider, for example, a community where the role of sperm in conception is not known and where people are unclear on what the actual roles of various body parts in biological reproduction are. Perhaps the belief is that a child gets conceived after a person with breasts has sex with a lot of people with various body parts and then has a dream of the right kind where the spirit gives them a child. Gender in this community is not likely to be tracking people with body parts presumed to be evidence of the actual role in biological reproduction, as this community has erroneous beliefs about it, but instead gender will, at best, track features taken to be evidence of the *believed* role. In this case, gender would not be the social significance of sex, but, at best, of what sex is taken to be. The problem with that is that this sort of account is not expressive of materialist commitments.

Haslanger is not faced with this exact problem, as she doesn't seem to think that sexes are classes defined by the relation in which they stand to the means of reproduction, but rather that sexes are biological categories. And persons aren't of a certain gender because of the actual relation in which they stand to the means of reproduction, but because of their perceived characteristics that are taken to be evidence of their role in biological reproduction. Haslanger does, however, face a related problem in hard cases, where a community is in error over the link between various body parts and bodily issues and their role in biological reproduction.

What is the problem? If Haslanger's justification for privileging the role in biological reproduction as the feature that matters to the assignment of gender is that hers is an actual class analysis where the actual relations people stand to the means of biological reproduction matters to the analysis, then there is a problem in cases where communities are in radical error as to what body parts and bodily issues and behaviors contribute what to the reproduction of the population. For in such cases the assignment of

---

[13] Thanks to Sally Haslanger for discussions about this.

gender ends up tracking something else entirely and the connection to the class analysis is lost. When that connection is lost, the justification for privileging the role in biological reproduction is also lost. There is thus an apparent tension between honoring both materialist feminist commitments and doing justice to the Beauvoirean slogan.

I will not discuss here how best to answer these worries. There may, for example, be other ways to justify privileging perceived roles in biological reproduction. My main point here is simply to draw out some of the key differences between Haslanger's views and my own, including the fact that Haslanger's is an articulation of a class analysis, where a commitment to materialist feminism is guiding the analysis.

It should be noted also that it is consistent with offering an account of gender as a social class to allow that there could be other phenomena in the vicinity that could be better captured with different analyses, which Haslanger has been upfront about. Haslanger's aim was to offer a materialist account of gender in the spirit of critical theory, and in a way that does justice to the post-Beauvoirean slogan. But there could be different accounts of gender offered that would capture other phenomena.[14]

While my account of gender differs in methodology from Haslanger, it does not differ in its aims. I agree with Haslanger about what phenomena need theoretical analysis, that oppression based on gender, race, and other categories is systematic and deeply entrenched ideologically, materially, as well as in our bodies. But the building blocks of the theory I use to attempt to explain all this are individual behavior and action. That might seem to be a limited range of tools, but it allows for great flexibility. In particular, it allows for a fairly simple way to account for the intersection of the various categories we inhabit, as we will see in chapter 6, when I complicate the picture told so far and discuss how it relates to objective and subjective identity. There is, on the other hand, no simple way to talk about the intersection of our social categories when one is offering a class analysis.

4.4.2 Linda Martín Alcoff

Linda Martín Alcoff offers an account of identity in her *Visible Identities: Race, Gender, and the Self* (2006), where the aim is to

---

[14] A class analysis may be a far cry from one that is needed for trans*liberatory politics. Haslanger's account has been charged with being trans*exclusionary (Jenkins 2016), but I think that is to miss its point, as should be clear from my discussion.

articulate a theoretically and practically useful notion of identity in the face of the widespread criticism of identity politics in academia and popular culture.

Alcoff takes social identity to have two components: our *public identity* is tied to our social location and how we are publicly perceived, classified, and interacted with. It corresponds to what I call "objective identity" in chapter 6. The other component, our *lived subjectivity*, need not map onto our public identity and can be experienced and conceptualized differently. The central positive project of Alcoff's book is to articulate an account of this lived subjectivity in a way that does justice to our way of being in the world: embodied subjectivities that are constituted through our public identities.

On Alcoff's view, our *sexed* identities are defined positionally and distinguished by their different possibilities as regard reproduction (2006: 172), but she thinks it is implausible to think that those objective differences with regard a person's possible roles in reproduction determine causally or in a linear way the culturally rich genders that exist across different contexts. The range of affective responses to, and interpretation of, reproductive possibilities are culturally shaped. Nevertheless, the objective differences in the range of possible reproductive roles one can take on always play some role in gender formation, whether a central or a peripheral one. Alcoff then looks to phenomenological and hermeneutic approaches to explore how this sexed identity is manifest in the lives of particular gendered individuals in specific social contexts (175).

Alcoff's project is to give an account of the lived experience of being gendered; mine is to give an account of gender as a social status. We are thus asking and answering different questions. But are the resulting theories compatible?

As on Alcoff's account, where our sexed identity is constrained by our actual relation to the range of possibilities as regards biological reproduction, and our gendered identity is similarly constrained by the cultural manifestation of that biological possibility, I read Alcoff as committed to materialist feminism, as well as a Beauvoirean distinction between sex and gender.

I agree with Alcoff that there can be material realities that put objective constraints on what role we can take in reproduction, but I don't think these objective constraints fall neatly into two sexed camps: I think each of us has various body parts and characteristics that determine the range of possible physical relations we can have to reproduction, and then various social and cultural elements also play a role in what our actual possible role can be.[15] And I think our gender (and our gender identity) is in many contexts divorced from our possible role in reproduction.

4.4.3 Charlotte Witt

Charlotte Witt offers an essentialist account of gender in her recent book, *The Metaphysics of Gender* (2011) that draws on Aristotle as well as feminist theory. This may appear a surprising project, given that as a result of decades of feminist critiques, "essentialism" has become a dirty word in feminist circles. However, as we read on, we realize that she is not arguing for the vilified form of essentialism, kind essentialism, that is, the view that to be a man (or woman) one need have some particular property that constitutes the essence of the kind and that explains and justifies the behavior of its members. Instead, she is offering a metaphysics of the social space we live in: what unifies and organizes the various social roles we occupy (parent, academic, politician, friend, student, etc.). Witt argues that gender is the function that unifies and organizes all our other social roles and is thus uniessential to us as social individuals.

The chief aim of Witt's account is to give a metaphysics of gender that can elucidate the centrality of gender in our lived experience, and she develops a framework to make sense of that centrality. Witt's gender essentialism is a view about the structure of social normativity, where social normativity is distinguished from other forms of normativity (including moral) and consists in the expectations, obligations, and allowances that the various social roles we occupy bring us. Witt thinks we are responsive to, and evaluated with respect to, these norms irrespective of whether we endorse them consciously or unconsciously (unlike what many would say about moral norms). She notes they often pull in different directions: my role as daughter may demand I avenge my father's death, my role as sister that I protect my brother at all costs. What unifies my many roles, however, is my gender. It also conditions my practical agency in the sense that gender expectations and obligations trump other ones, often making it impossible to fulfill the obligations of the various social roles adequately. The gendering of our social roles is largely to blame.

The central claim in her account of the pervasiveness of the gendering of our social norms is that, as a matter of fact, in Western late

---

[15] Think of the societal restriction (institutional or communal) on reproduction by people with particular features: having "homosexual tendencies", having mental disabilities, being a poor woman, etc.

capitalist societies like the United States, gender is *uniessential* to social individuals, and that is what explains the pervasiveness of gender. Let us flesh this out.

First, for a function to be uniessential to an entity is for it to unify and organize all the parts of that individual into the whole that is the individual. For example, the time-telling function unifies and organizes all the tiny metal parts (hands, spring, gears, etc.) into the whole that is the watch itself. Similarly, the sheltering function unifies and organizes all the planks of a wooden house into the entity that is the house itself.

Gender, understood in this way, is a function that organizes all the parts of a social individual into the social individual it is. The parts in question are all the other social roles the social individual occupies: parent, friend, professor, child, colleague, and so on. Gender (man, woman) is a megasocial role that unifies all the other social roles into the agent that is the social individual. Being a woman, a parent, and so on is to occupy a social position, with which come norms of behavior. The social individual is the entity that occupies all these social positions, the bearer of these social properties, if you will.

The social individual is distinct from the human organism and the person, because the social individual stands in social relations essentially, but human organisms and persons do so only accidentally. Similarly, the person is distinct from the human organism and the social individual because the person has the capacity to take a first-person perspective on itself essentially, but the human organism and the social individual only have that accidentally. Finally, the human organism has certain biological features essentially, but the person and the social individual does so only accidentally.

What determines whether you occupy a certain social position? On Witt's view, being a man and being a woman are social positions—social statuses, if you will—that come with social norms, and people are responsive to and evaluated with respect to these norms irrespective of their self-understanding or their endorsing these norms. Whether they occupy these positions or not depends on their being socially recognized. The social recognition includes recognition of other members of the group, institutional recognition as exemplified by a birth certificate, driver's licenses, marriage licenses, and other forms of group recognition such as initiation rituals.

Witt also privileges biological reproduction in her account of gender, and her account is an explanation of why gendering is so pervasive and why it trumps other social roles. It is because of its relation to biological reproduction, which is a necessary function. I have engaged critically with Witt's view elsewhere (2012); here I simply address the claim regarding the relation between gender and reproduction. Let us look at the central analogy: engendering is to reproduction as dining is to feeding.

The main idea is, and it is an attractive one, that there are basic functions that humans need to perform, but that need and the underlying material conditions radically underdetermine the form that the performance of that function can take. I take it that the engendering function and the dining function are at the social level, and reproduction and feeding are at the biological level. The analogy goes like this: We have the need to eat. That need and the material conditions we find ourselves in radically underdetermine the way that need gets satisfied. Dining practices are social conventions set up to respond to the biological need we have to eat. Similarly, we have a need to reproduce, but that need and the material conditions we find ourselves in radically underdetermine the way that need gets met. The system of gender relations is the social conventions set up to respond to our biological need for reproduction.

There are some disanalogies here. The organism can be said to have a need to feed itself or be fed, but it doesn't seem that the organism has a similar need to reproduce. If it did, then the people who do not reproduce would not be meeting some basic need, and that seems implausible. We might want to say that the population has a need to reproduce itself, where "population" is defined in purely biological terms, and where we then say that various social reproductive practices are ways of responding to that need. But if we say that, then it seems that the two genders Witt thinks are needed at the social level to respond to the biological need are not enough. For there are many other roles played by individuals that serve a reproductive function for the population, and on which the health of the population depends, including priests, caregivers of various sorts, teachers, and so on.

Even if we want to restrict gender roles to roles in the reproduction economy, so that individuals who do not partake in it by providing the biological material don't get assigned a gender, we run into another problem. Witt's view is that gender unifies and organizes all our other social roles; it would follow that the agency of priests and others who would lack gender would lack normative unity.

So while I agree with Witt that being of a gender is a social position, conferred onto us (as I would put it), I don't think that the base property in the conferral is solely a perceived role in the system of biological reproduction. I think that is sometimes what is going on, but often it is not.

Frequently the base feature in the conferral of the status of being a woman, man, or some other gender is the mere presence of some body parts, presumed sexual orientation, self-presentation, self-identification, and the like. So I think Witt's account of gender is too narrow.

But the other point of disagreement is the role of gender in underwriting our practical social agency. I think there is something else that has to do it. But I don't think we need some principle of normative unity. I think all we need is intentionality and practical rationality. We need to be able to form attitudes about things, be it the food we want to eat or a film we want to see. And we need to have the capacity for practical rationality, namely, to take the means toward our ends. Human organisms are capable of this, as are other animals, such as dogs. And both humans and dogs are social beings.

On my account of gender, there is no essential link to biology or reproduction. Gender is a social status conferred upon us in particular contexts, where the base property or properties may or may not be biological or reproductive. My account of gender is thus a clear alternative to Witt's. That being said, my main objective is to offer a general framework to account for all social categories and give an account of what it is for a property to be socially significant. The scope of my work is thus broader than Witt's. However, there is a clear affinity with, and indebtedness to, Witt's work, because of primary interest to her is what she calls "social" normativity (as opposed to moral, legal, institutional, logical, etc.), which I think of as *communal* normativity in this book and which plays a large role in the maintenance of communal social categories.

All the theorists I have just discussed—Alcoff, Haslanger, and Witt— share that accompanying their account of gender is an explanation for why gender functions like it does. Both Alcoff and Haslanger have materialist commitments, and relations to the means of reproduction play a role in explaining one's social position (Haslanger) and social identity (Alcoff). And Witt offers an Aristotelian explanation in terms of an essential function: we have an essential need to reproduce, and gender plays a role in fulfilling that need.

I offer neither an explanation nor a justification of why certain features serve as base features for the conferral of a social status in this book. It is, however, compatible with my story that material conditions shape our consciousness and influence which features we find salient in some (even all) the contexts we travel. But my account is compatible with other explanations, too.

4.4.4 Talia Bettcher

While the three theorists I have discussed so far all link gender to biological reproduction in one way or another, the last one, whose views I will compare with mine, does not, and has other aims.

Talia Bettcher (2013) argues that an approach to the meaning of gender terms according to which words like "woman" have different meanings in different cultural contexts is best equipped to make sense of trans experiences, practices, and politics. What does Bettcher's view of gender come to, and how does it differ from the view advocated here?

Bettcher distinguishes her "multiple-meanings" position from a "single-meaning" view, as well as semantic contextualism. On a single-meaning view, there is a feature or set of features that give the meaning of a gender term irrespective of the context. Given that there is no feature or set of features that all and only women share, a single-meaning view of gender terms needs to resort to a family resemblance or cluster view to make sense of the phenomena. In both cases, trans women come out as marginal cases of womanhood and thus are not good starting points for trans liberatory politics. On semantic contextualism,[16] one can be a woman in one context and not in another, because the standards of relevance to the paradigm case vary with context. The problem for using semantic contextualism for trans liberatory politics is, though, that the trans activist cannot, on this view, deny that there are some contexts in which she isn't a woman (even if she is a woman in some other contexts). On Bettcher's multiple-meanings view, however, there is a meaning of "woman" that is operative in the dominant culture and then there is a meaning of "woman" operative in the trans subculture. The use of the term "woman" as operating in the dominant culture has no application with respect to individuals in the subculture, except as enforced on them by institutional and brute force. The dominant meanings belong to gender practices—a form of life—that persons in the subculture repudiate, just as persons who aren't Catholic might meet all the criteria for being a sinner according to the Catholic church, but nonetheless aren't sinners as they don't participate in a form of life in which there are sins and sinners.

Bettcher seeks a semantics of gender terms that can support the metaphysical claim that trans women are women. I take my project to be friendly to trans liberatory politics, but I have different aims from Bettcher. I'm not giving a semantics of gender terms. And while I am giving a metaphysics

---

[16] This view is discussed by Jennifer Saul (2012).

of gender, given the metaphysics I offer, the metaphysics is not going to settle who *ought* to be a woman. I'm giving an account of what it is for gender to be a social feature. And if gender is a social feature, how is it constructed and maintained? And on the account I offer, the question, "But are you really a woman?" is a bad question. There is no such thing as being a real woman or natural woman (*pace* popular song lyrics). There is just having the status of being a woman in a particular context. And then there is of course the normative question: should X be a woman in context C? And that requires a substantive normative enquiry to answer.

The concern I have about Bettcher's account is that it is not clear to me how we can critique forms of life (or gender practices) and argue that one form is better or more just than another, if the meanings and justification of our gender attribution is grounded in the gender practices in question. This worry is analogous to worries about how we can critique an alternative conceptual scheme, or a scientific theory, if such criticism always has to be made from within one scheme or theory. Catherine Z. Elgin (1996) discusses these sorts of challenges and the ways in which one can evaluate different theories without assuming "a view from nowhere", but it is not clear to me whether Bettcher can avail herself of those strategies. I will, however, not linger on that issue here.

4.5 LGBTQ Status

The conferralist framework can help illuminate the status of LGBTQ people, both institutionally and communally. LGBTQ people get conferred onto them institutional statuses for the purposes of criminal law, civil law, and antidiscrimination law, as well as private institutional rules and regulations such as that of the Boy Scouts of America and the Catholic Church. There is also a robust history of the institutional medical status of the "homosexual" and other "deviants." What count as base properties for the conferral of the status of homosexual, transsexual, transgender, trans*, queer, and so on, varies with context. For the Catholic Church, for example, being taken to have same-sex desires or thoughts may be enough to get the status homosexual conferred onto you. For a criminal status, you may need to have been caught in the act of having sex with someone of the same sex (notwithstanding that it took place in the sanctity of your own home). In certain legal contexts, it is only possible to be a criminal homosexual if you are a man, as sex between two women is not legally criminalized (perhaps because it is unfathomable, it doesn't even register legally). All this is to say that the base properties for the conferral of the various institutional statuses that fall under the LGBTQ umbrella can vary considerably, and the constraints and enablements that come with the conferral can as well.

To be gay, or trans*, or queer *communally* functions much the same as does gender, in that in different contexts you can have such a status conferred onto you if you are taken to have the base property. In one context, for example, someone may get conferred onto them the status of being gay because of self-presentation or mannerism, in another because of self-professed (sexual) political affiliation. The communal property of being a lesbian, for example, is deeply context dependent, with many possible base properties: having a sexual desire for another woman, having fallen in love with another woman, having acted on desires for another woman, having acted on the love for another woman, living with another woman as a partner, living openly with another as a partner, affiliating oneself with the lesbian movement, considering oneself as a lesbian, and so on. A person can have one of these base properties without having the others. And being taken to have the relevant base property in a context confers the status of lesbian on you in that context.

The constraints and enablements vary with contexts. In the context of a postsurgery hospital room in North Carolina, you can be neglected as a patient, the nurse can "forget" to call in a time-sensitive prescription, and treat you as if you have a highly contagious moral disease. And there can be enablements: persons who have suffered discrimination and mistreatment on the basis of some other features they are taken to have might be more open to you and what you have to say on the matter because they assume you are an ally and "get" what is at issue.

4.6 Interpreting Disputes

As I write this in the spring of 2017, not only do I observe daily the conferralist framework in action, as people are being assigned a social status on the basis of what ethnic or racial heritage and sex they are taken to have, I also observe intense disputes over what it is to be of a certain gender. The movement for LGBTQ equality, including the marriage equality movement and the trans* movement, has brought into relief conflicting attitudes regarding gender in particular.

What sort of question is "what is a woman?" and can the conferralist offer an answer to what we are doing when we are asking that question?

I argue in this book that sex and racial categories are social categories, just as gender, LGBTQ, and religious categories are. These are social features, conferred by human beings. What, then, is going on when there are disputes over what it is to be a woman and whether a person is a woman? On my view, disputes over what it is to be a woman are disputes over what feature should be the base property for the conferral of the institutional or communal status *woman* in a particular context.

Let's consider the dispute between Trans Exclusionary Radical Feminists (TERFs) and Transwomen. TERFs promoted women-only events, such as the Michigan Womyn's Festival, where the definition of "woman" deliberately excluded transwomen. Transwomen, on the other hand, insist that transwomen are women. This is a case where the TERFs want the base property for the conferral of the status woman in a particular context to be *born with a vagina*, and transwomen want *self-identification* to be the base property. What is to settle the issue?

We cannot hope to somehow find out what the real facts about gender are to settle the matter.[17] The real facts about gender are that they are constructions, but that does not settle the matter. They are creatures of our own making, and we need to ask ourselves whether the creatures we live with are justifiable. Are the distinctions that are drawn morally and politically justifiable? In this case, what is the justification for conferring woman status only on people born with a vagina in a particular context? Does that justification hold up to scrutiny, with respect to that context, and with respect to potential other ones? Similarly, we ask for the justification for having self-identification be the base property for the conferral in the particular context we are concerned with, and potential other contexts. Does that justification hold up to scrutiny?

On the account I offer, the question *what is a woman?* is thus revealed to ultimately demand an answer to a different question: *who should be a woman?* Similarly for other social categories.

I give similar answers to the question of what is to settle matters over disputes over race, ethnicity, religion, sexual orientation, disability, and so on. What are these categories for? Can the base properties for the conferral of the various statuses be justified for the particular statuses and contexts intended? And the related question: can we justify that a certain feature is socially significant at all in a context? While we need to examine carefully each and every case, the answer to the last question is in many cases a resounding NO.

---

[17] Here I am in agreement with Robin Dembroff (2016) in MS.

There are many social categories whose existence may be unjustified. These social categories should not exist because the feature that serves as the base property for the conferral of them should not be socially significant.

4.7 Response Dependence Again: Merit

I have claimed that figuring out the metaphysical facts about gender, for example, would not settle the question, which is very much a live question in societies such as the United States today: what is a woman? And the reason is that being a woman is a social status, and figuring that out is only the beginning of enquiry. Of course, we could answer the question *what is a woman?* empirically: in this and that context, the base property for the conferral of the status is sex assignment, or the presence of a vagina, or self-identification. But that doesn't *settle* the matter. Is the base property in question justified? Given the status that gets conferred onto a person, is the base property for the conferral justifiable? And further: is it justifiable at all to confer said status on a person?

Given that my analysis of the metaphysics of social categories reveals that there are deep normative questions that need to be answered with respect to the question whether the presence of a certain property merits differential treatment, the reader may be surprised that in chapter 1, when I discussed various frameworks for making sense of social properties, I dismissed response-dependence theories without much ado. Was that a mistake?

In chapter 1, I discussed a certain version of a response-dependence view that involves inducing certain responses in subjects (or a disposition to cause such responses). But the response-dependence literature includes a lot of other types of theories. In particular, it includes the following idea:[18]

X is P iff X merits response R in subject S in context C.

For example:

X is a woman iff X merits the response in S that X be treated in manner M

---

[18] Examples of such an approach may be McDowell 1983 and 1985.

Given that my metaphysical investigation reveals that we have to answer deep normative questions, doesn't it seem that a meriting-response account of social properties is a good contender?

I don't think so. A response-dependence account of this variety is designed to answer a different question, namely, under what conditions X is P, where P is a normative property. It is thus designed to answer a certain sort of normative question. It may even be that a version of it could be brought to bear on answering the normative question my book reveals we need answered, that is, ought X be a woman in C? But if so, it is up to a different task than mine. It then takes up the gauntlet from where I threw it and attempts to answer the normative question by appealing to *merit*. Whatever the promise of such an account for answering the normative questions we need answering, it isn't up to the task of giving the metaphysics of social properties. For people have various social properties, including ones that are subordinate statuses without meriting that treatment at all. The merit-response account specifically answers the question when the conferral of a status is right: it is when the subject merits it.

CHAPTER 5 | Conferralism about Other Social Categories

IN THIS CHAPTER, I apply the conferralist framework to some of the other "usual suspects", that is, to some of the other categories that are protected classes in various jurisdictions, such as race, religion, and disability. A fuller picture of the construction of the various categories would require more engagement with empirical field work on those categories, but I hope that what I say in this chapter gives the reader an adequate understanding of how such accounts would proceed. And, equally importantly, I hope that the sketches in this chapter add more flesh to the skeletal framework offered in this book.

5.1 Institutional Race in America

Research in genetics and biology of the last few decades has, to my mind, completely decimated the idea that racial categories are biological.[1] People don't belong to racial categories because of some genetic or biological feature about them. Race is not a scientifically respectable explanatory category, as no natural phenomena can be explained by appealing to race (as opposed to some notion of a population with a shared history or a kindred notion). A host of social phenomena can, on the other hand, be explained by reference to a person's race, ranging from the statistical likelihood of becoming a prison inmate to completing a college degree or being shot by police. Races are social categories.

There have been times in American history when racial categories have been institutional categories, as I have characterized them, and encoded

---

[1] UNESCO 1967; Zack 1993; Appiah 1996.

in law. Vestiges of that still remain and play a larger role than might first appear. When we fill out official documents, we are asked to identify our race. There has in fact been a shift in the last few decades, as now we are asked what race we identify with, if any. Gone are the days where some official classifies us as belonging to a race, based on documents to the effect that we had ancestors known to be of a certain race. By all appearances, nowadays we get conferred onto us an institutional race status on the basis of our self-identification. But appearances are misleading.

Consider the case of Rachel Dolezal. She is an American civil rights activist and former president of the Spokane chapter of the National Association for the Advancement of Colored People. She resigned from her presidency of the NAACP chapter in 2015 under allegations that she had fabricated aspects of her personal history, including her race. She identified as black, but people felt betrayed to learn that she was not of African American ancestry. She was accused of being an imposter when her parents came out and claimed she wasn't black. Why wasn't she? Can the conferralist framework help us understand this situation?[2]

First, we might want to consider whether races are institutional or communal categories. I'm inclined to think that there are institutional racial categories, operating in many different institutional contexts,[3] and on top of that there is a variety of context-dependent communal categories.

That there are remnants of institutional racial categories should not be controversial. When we fill out official forms, we are asked to identify with one or more racial categories. For instance, when I applied for my US citizenship in 2016, I was asked to identify gender, ethnicity, race, hair color, and eye color for the purposes of a "criminal records check."[4] Not only are racial categories used in attempts to rectify current and past injustices, such as when certain scholarships are only available to people of a certain racial category; they are also used when classifying people accused of crimes, those needing governmental assistance, or living in certain neighborhoods, among other things. How is that "classified" information then used? It is

---

[2] There are a lot of questions that arise when considering Dolezal's case. I am here chiefly focused on the metaphysics. For some thoughtful writing on various issues surrounding Dolezal's case see, e.g, Oluo 2017; Krisnamurti 2017.

[3] The institutional categories at work in each institutional context can vary, depending on the law or policy at work.

[4] The categories were as follows: gender (Male/Female); ethnicity (Hispanic or Latino / Not Hispanic or Latino); race (White / Asian / Black or African American / American Indian or Alaska Native / Native Hawaiian or Other Pacific Islander); hair color (Black/Brown/Blonde/Grey/White/Red/Sandy/Bald [No Hair]); eye color (Brown/Blue/Green/Hazel/Gray/Black/Pink/Maroon/Other). Application for Naturalization. Form N-400.

used in the allocation of resources at local, state, and national levels, and in law enforcement. For example, will the city council have the roads in a particular neighborhood fixed? Will it put up sidewalks? Will they improve public transportation in that area? The answers to these questions may depend on how the residents get classified and how the people in power view those classifications. While the official justification for asking people to self-identify with a certain race is to monitor discrimination and injustice,[5] that information is also used in other ways. And because racial classifications are used in official ways in the allocation of resources, and not simply for monitoring purposes, institutional racial categories are not just a thing of the past; they are alive and well.

The various governmental and nongovernmental agencies and institutions confer institutional racial categories on individuals for their own purposes, but the authorities rely on our self-reporting. What is the status of these self-identifications? Are they the base properties for the conferral? Consider what the US Census has written regarding race on its website:

> The U.S. Census Bureau must adhere to the 1997 Office of Management and Budget (OMB) standards on race and ethnicity which guide the Census Bureau in classifying written responses to the race question:
>
> **White**—A person having origins in any of the original peoples of Europe, the Middle East, or North Africa.
>
> **Black or African American**—A person having origins in any of the Black racial groups of Africa.
>
> **American Indian or Alaska Native**—A person having origins in any of the original peoples of North and South America (including Central America) and who maintains tribal affiliation or community attachment.
>
> **Asian**—A person having origins in any of the original peoples of the Far East, Southeast Asia, or the Indian subcontinent including, for example, Cambodia, China, India, Japan, Korea, Malaysia, Pakistan, the Philippine Islands, Thailand, and Vietnam.

---

[5] From the US Census website: "Reasons for Collecting Information on Race:

Information on race is required for many Federal programs and is critical in making policy decisions, particularly for civil rights. States use these data to meet legislative redistricting principles. Race data also are used to promote equal employment opportunities and to assess racial disparities in health and environmental risks" (United States Census Bureau, "Race: About This Topic," last revised January 23, 2018, https://www.census.gov/topics/population/race/about.html).

Native Hawaiian or Other Pacific Islander—A person having origins in any of the original peoples of Hawaii, Guam, Samoa, or other Pacific Islands.

The 1997 OMB standards permit the reporting of more than one race. An individual's response to the race question is based upon self-identification. [6]

I read institutional racial categories that rely on the OMB standard such that they get conferred onto you by authorities using the information about your self-identification unless there is evidence to the contrary. Your self-identification is not really the base property for the conferral, but is taken as *evidence* for your having the base property, which is a certain biological genealogy with ancestry in a certain region of the world, as the definitions provided above attest to.

There was a time in US history when institutional racial categories were conferred much like my conferral account of sex categories. A person's race was recorded on that person's birth certificate by officials shortly after birth. Many US states still have race recorded on the birth certificate, and they are often recorded by a nurse on the basis of a cursory look at the mother.[7] Many states, however, avowedly only record race for statistical purposes and rely on people's own self-identification. Yet this information is not only used for monitoring, but for other purposes, such as resource allocation and law enforcement. For this reason, we have functioning institutional racial categories in the United States. But the paradigm conferralist story of institutional status doesn't quite seem to capture how they get constructed.

These seem to be the facts: the OMB committee decides they want to track the distribution of resources and various other sociological data using five racial categories. They don't want these categories imposed on people, so people are to self-identity. These categories then also get used for decision-making, and not merely monitoring.

Consider this analogy. You are a theater director and you are putting on *Macbeth*. You have to work with the troupe at the repertory theater who has hired you and cannot hire an outside actor, but otherwise you have completely free rein in assigning roles. You call them all together for the first meeting and say, "Sam, you will be Macbeth, Kim, Lady Macbeth", and so on. You have the authority to assign them roles, and you do. In

---

[6] United States Census Bureau, "Race: About This Topic," last revised January 23, 2018, https://www.census.gov/topics/population/race/about.html.
[7] Sink 1997.

assigning roles, you are not quite attempting to "get things right", although you are trying to match the actor's interpretive and expressive skills with the character in question.

Let us now consider the case where you are deeply uncomfortable with asserting your authority as the director (this may not always work well in practice!) and that you don't want to assign the actors their roles. They are to claim them. As it turns out, in this case, they each claim exactly the roles that you assigned in the previous case. Sam claimed Macbeth, Kim Lady Macbeth, and so on. But you did not confer the roles onto them in the same way as in the first case.

There are many things that stay the same in the second scenario. In particular, the actors play their roles, which come with constraints and enablements, and there are norms that govern the interaction between the characters on the stage, as well as the script that needs to be followed. But the status of the actors was not conferred by you; it was assumed by them.

The assignment of institutional racial categories in the United States in the beginning of the twenty-first century is a bit like the role assignment in a play where a director is uncomfortable with authority: the director brings in the roles available and hopes the actors themselves identify with the characters. The OMB committee does something similar: it decides that there should be five racial categories as well as the base properties for each, but then it is uncomfortable with people being assigned their racial status, so they hope people self-identify—which they do, by and large. The twist is just that these categories do get used down the line in ways where authority is exercised, such as when the police use racial demographic information in their law enforcement, or when the transportation agency uses the same in their investment in a new metro line.

For these reasons, I say that there are remnants of fully fledged institutional racial categories in the United States, but that because of the history of the use of racial categories in discriminatory institutions and practices, there is extreme discomfort in assigning people institutional racial status.[8]

Let's think more about the role of authority in these cases. Do we want to say that the authorities delegate the authority to the individuals who self-identify in this case? Consider you, the uncomfortable director, again. You do have de jure authority to change the assignment if you think it's not going very well or if someone is miscast. Of course, you may not have de facto authority. For instance, your actors may sense your discomfort with

---

[8] For discussion of race classifications in the United States, see, e.g., Davis 2001; Omi and Winant 1994; Snipp 2003; Prewitt 2005.

assuming authority and disrespect your authority for that reason. Or they may disrespect your authority for some prejudicial reason (they are sexist, ableist, racist, transphobic, islamophobic, etc.). But let's put these aside. The point is that even if you are uncomfortable with exercising your authority and you want the actors to find their roles themselves without your having to assign them, you could revoke their choices. I like to think of this sort of case as a *latent* use of authority: you ask people to take on roles themselves, but in the background is your authority to confer the roles onto them should they not comply. Whether you exercise that authority if they don't comply is then a different matter. If you are directing a play, you need actors for each role, so you will assign the role if the actor is reluctant. In the case of various institutions in the United States, including state, federal, local, and private ones, the cost may be too high for them to confer status onto those who don't identify.

Consider the case of Rachel Dolezal again. Much earlier than the NAACP scandal, she had been assumed to be African American in her MFA application to Howard University, a historically black college, and had been given a scholarship reserved for African Americans for the first year.[9] When school authorities met her, they judged her not to have African American ancestry and started to treat her as white institutionally. She then sued them for discrimination on the basis of race. She alleged that she had been discriminated against with regard to scholarships and other opportunities because she was white.

This seems to me a case where people are allowed to self-identify . . . unless they don't identify *correctly*. Rachel Dolezal had to exhibit features presumed to be evidence for African American ancestry. Having African American ancestry was the base property for the conferral. And if Dolezal exhibited features that contradicted the assumption that she had African American ancestry, then her status was revoked. This case is analogous to that of the director who reassigns roles when they don't like what the actors have assumed. Pat just can't be Lady Macbeth!

For the reasons that have emerged in the above examples, I think that institutional racial categories in the United States are conferred using latent authority in the manner we have discussed. The body that would have the authority to confer the institutional categories delegates this authority to individual agents who are asked to self-identify. They are in effect asked to

---

[9] Barnes 2015.

bear witness to their racial status, and they are taken at their word, unless it gets contested, in which case the authority may revoke or change the status.

Here is the schema for the institutional racial categories currently operating in many institutional contexts in the US:[10]

> **Property:** being of the institutional race R, for example, Black or African American, White or Caucasian, Asian, Native Hawaiian or Other Pacific Islander, American Indian or Native Alaskan.
> **Who:** legal and political authorities, drawing on self-identification in official documents
> **What:** the recording of a race identification in official files and documents
> **When:** in each context where the official document plays a role in decision making
> **Base property:** supposed actual geographic ancestry, but the evidence for it is self-identification

Let me address some worries. First, why think that racial categories are conferred on people by authorities? Doesn't it seem that people are themselves taking on membership in these categories? Also, here we have a case where some governmental committee in 1997 decided that there should be these five racial categories. It seems that the committee brought these categories into being, not individual authorities that confer racial status onto individuals.

Let me address the second worry first and start by spelling it out a bit more. In this book, I am claiming that the conferralist framework can be used to articulate a certain conception of social construction that explains how social categories are constructed and maintained. But here it seems that the OMB committee in 1997 made the executive decision that there be five racial categories, and which features defined each. Doesn't it seem that the OMB committee brought these categories into being with something akin to what Austin (1975) calls an "exercitive act" and Searle (1969) a "declaration"?

> OMB Committee: "Let there be five official racial categories in the United States: Black or African American, White or Caucasian, Asian, Native Hawaiian or Other Pacific Islander, American Indian or Native Alaskan!"

---

[10] Official US documents such as the US Census and the applications for citizenship use the racial categories designated by the Office of Management and Budget (OMB) in 1997. Individual states and localities may use a more elaborate set of distinctions, but the profile of the institutional status is similar.

Doesn't this seem to be how the institutional racial categories were constructed, not in the way that I suggest?

It is true that the OMB committee specifies what racial categories there should be for various purposes and what the base properties for the conferral should be. But how does anyone come to have the status? For us to have a status, it needs to be assigned in some way.

Compare with the baseball case again. The rulebook for baseball says that a pitch is a strike if it travels through the strike zone, say. The rulebook, in effect, specifies the base properties for the conferral of a strike. But how does anything get to have that status? It needs to be a pitch that is judged by the umpire to have the base property. With that, a new status comes into being and a new baseball fact is born.

Similarly for marriage. The law states the conditions under which persons can get married and to whom and how they should go about doing it. Then A and B fill out forms, pay a fee, and under oath and in the presence of witnesses vow to enter into a union. The justice confers the status of being married onto them on the basis of their taking A and B to have fulfilled all the preconditions and played their part in the ceremony adequately. They are not married by meeting certain conditions. They get married by being taken to meet the conditions and having the status conferred on that basis.

Compare the OMB committee to the playwright who writes a script that never gets produced: no actors take on their roles, no plot unfolds on stage. Unless the play gets produced, there is no performance. No actors inhabit any roles, no actors relate to another in their roles, no one laughs or cries.

The OMB have produced a script. But that isn't enough. The organizations and agencies have to stage the play. People don't live by categories they don't inhabit. How do they get to inhabit those roles? The director may have clear directives for how the roles should be assigned and what the base properties for the assignment should be. But our director is uncomfortable with assigning the roles and so wants the actors to self-identify. Once the actors do, the rehearsals can begin.

Similarly, the OMB standard provides legal directives for what categories there should be and what the base properties for the conferrals should be. The conferral takes place as a latent conferral through self-identification.

I now want to address a worry regarding the suggestion that a feature may not be the base property but rather the evidence for the base property. How can we tell? Also, in chapter 1 I distinguished between my conferralist account and a Searlean constitution account by saying that if persons got conferred onto them a certain status, say that of being married, then they were married when they had that status, even if their status might later be revoked when authorities discovered they were already married to someone else or failed to meet some other of the prerequisites for being married.

On a Searlean constitution account of being married (being R counts as being M in C), if individuals aren't R at all, but were merely faking it, they are not married and never were, even though they were treated institutionally as married, even for forty years. What exactly is the conferralist story? What precisely are the base properties for the conferral of being married? Is it the features R (not being married to someone else, etc.)? Or is it the documents attesting to features R? Let us say that it is the features R themselves and let us suppose the judge judges the couple to have the features when in fact they don't. They then get the status *married*.

Consider the following case. Alex and Chris want to get married. Unbeknownst to Alex, Chris is actually married to three other people who are scattered around the world. Chris, on the other hand, has a document in the country where they intend to get married, and on the document it says that Chris is single. Alex and Chris get married. Now, did Chris meet the requirements R since they had the legal status *single* in the country where they were? The answer to that depends on the precise requirements R. In some contexts, it could be that it is the legal status single in the country in question that matters, in others that the person not be married to others anywhere in the world, and the legal document merely serves as evidence for that. But this can be quite tricky, and there could be hard cases where a court might have to settle what the base properties are. For instance, Chris might be a man married to a man in Iceland, but North Carolina does not recognize marriages between two men, and therefore treats him as single even though North Carolina generally accepts the marriage status of people married in Iceland. Chris might also be married to two women in Morocco, but, again, North Carolina does not recognize polygamous marriages, even though it generally accepts the marriage status of people married in Morocco. But let's put aside such interesting complications and take a case of willfully attempting to pass as meeting requirements R. Let's say that Chris is a man and he married Margaret (a woman) in Australia who has since disappeared into the Australian Outback and he hasn't been able to find her to divorce her. He decides to just lie and claim he's single. Now Chris and Alex marry and live together happily or not for thirty years until Alex dies scuba-diving in the Caribbean at the age of seventy. Margaret suddenly shows up on Chris's doorstep in San Francisco. Is Chris married to Margaret? Were Alex and Chris married for thirty years? My inclination is to say that yes, Alex and Chris were married for thirty years and that, yes, Chris is still married to Margaret. Chris managed to marry Alex even though he wasn't supposed to, as he was already married to Margaret.[11]

I'm also inclined to think that the base properties are the requirements R, and not the documents that attest to Chris's meeting the requirements. The test of that is that if someone can bring proof that Chris is already married, say, even though he has the documents that attest to his being single, his newly married status is revoked. More generally: a feature is a base property if evidence to the effect that someone lacks the feature trumps the presence of documents normally accepted as evidence. A feature is mere evidence of a base feature if further considerations can trump the evidence, even if true. Consider self-identification on official forms. Suppose someone self-identifies on a form as a female when applying to a single-sex school for girls. When asked to produce a birth certificate, the certificate says "male", and that person is not allowed to attend the school. That is a case where the base property was sex assignment on a birth certificate, even though self-identification was used as defeasible evidence. Consider also self-identification of race on the form. If one self-identifies as an American Indian, but it comes out that one has no affiliation with any tribe, that status gets revoked. The revoking of a status can reveal two things: where the authority lies, and what serves as a base property as opposed to evidence thereof.

5.2 Communal Racial Categories

Apart from the institutional racial categories that get conferred and used for various official purposes, there are also context-dependent communal racial categories. What the base properties are in each context can vary. Sometimes, it is biological genealogy with ancestry in sub-Saharan Africa, or Europe, or East Asia, as is in the institutional case, but sometimes that isn't enough, or not relevant. Consider this scenario:

> Two young men look similar enough in terms of skin color, bone structure and physique, that one could take them for brothers. Mike was born and raised in the United States, Emmanuel in Togo, but the latter has recently

---

[11] What precisely we say about this does depend on the precise base property in question and the legal code regarding such a status. But even in cases where the marriage gets revoked or even annulled, that doesn't change the fact that Alex and Chris functioned socially as married for thirty years. They have that status for thirty years. And that is what my account is to capture.

moved to the United States. They are sitting by their fire on Ocean Beach in San Francisco when they see a police car pulling in. Mike says, "Come on, let's go! The police are here." Emmanuel doesn't see a problem: "But, we are not doing anything illegal. We are just hanging out!" Mike then replies, "You don't get it, Emmanuel. You aren't black the way I am black."

Mike wasn't talking about the color of Emmanuel's skin, and he wasn't talking about his ancestry. He was talking about that Emmanuel had just moved to the United States from Togo and he doesn't yet know how to navigate this new environment as a young African American man, including what sorts of scenarios to avoid. The concepts he uses to make sense of himself, others, and the environment, as well as his body language and the way he is embodied in space, have not yet been adapted to the new reality that is his new home in the United States. He does not share in the collected memory of past treatment and hasn't developed the navigational and coping skills to deal with that treatment. In this context, Mike does not afford Emmanuel status as black, for the purposes of judging the danger in the situation correctly, because Emmanuel doesn't have the navigational skills of one who understands the dangers of sitting by the fire on a beach while appearing male and of African ancestry. The base property in this context is having the navigational skills of a black young man.

Communal racial status can change with context. When Mike and Emmanuel are handcuffed by the police for sitting on a beach eating hot dogs, they are both young black men. Awareness of history, navigational skill, or identification does not matter. Accent does not matter. Only the color of their skin does.

Charles Mills (1998) discusses seven different possible criteria for racial self-identification and identification by others: bodily appearance, ancestry, self-awareness of ancestry, public awareness of ancestry, culture, experience, and subjective identification. It is the identification by others that is relevant to the communal status, and all of the features Mills mentions can serve as base properties (there may also be others). Here is the schema for the communal racial statuses:

Conferred property: being of communal race R, for example, Black, White, Asian, Native American, and so on. The number and specificity of options varies with context. For example, in one context Asian may be an option, in another, Korean or Hmong

Who: the subjects with communal standing in the particular context

What: the perception of the subject S that the person have the base property P

When: in some particular context

Base property: the base property P, for example, bodily appearance, ancestry, self-awareness of ancestry, public awareness of ancestry, culture, experience, subjective identification

Mike may be Black in one context, but not in another, because in different contexts different features are the basis for the conferral. There may be contexts where self-identification is a base property, but those contexts seem to be not as prevalent as the context in which gender self-identification is the basis. There is a sharp contrast between gender and race in the United States in that regard.[12]

5.3 Race in Other Contexts

Our discussion about race so far has been focused on the United States. Generally speaking, the conferralist model can be used to cast light on institutional and communal social categories, but the specifics will vary with contexts. Consider race and ethnicity in the United Kingdom, for example.[13] The institutional categories in the United Kingdom are sustained in similar ways as in the United States: there is an authority that announces a number of categories to be used and asks people on official documents and in surveys to self-identify. The Census categories are used by the Census, as well as various other bodies, but some agencies and institutions use their own categories, for example the police. What is striking in the UK context is that the term "race" seems to have been substituted for "ethnicity", but racial distinctions permeate the seemingly ethnic groupings. For example, in England, the classifications recommended by the Office for National Statistics (ONS) are as follows:

White (1. English/Welsh/Scottish/Northern Irish/British; 2. Irish; 3. Gypsy or Irish Traveller; 4. Any other White background)

---

[12] Compare the Dolezal case to that of a transwoman who identifies as a woman. I note the explosive discussion in wake of the "*Hypatia* affair."

[13] See Classifications: Office for National Statistics, "Classifications and Harmonisation," accessed May 24, 2017, https://www.ons.gov.uk/methodology/classificationsandstandards.

Mixed/Multiple ethnic groups (5. White and Black Caribbean; 6. White and Black African; 7. White and Asian; 8. Any other Mixed/ Multiple ethnic background)

Asian/Asian British (9. Indian; 10. Pakistani; 11. Bangladeshi; 12. Chinese; 13. Any other Asian background)

Black/African/Caribbean/Black British (14. African; 15. Caribbean; 16. Any other Black/African/Caribbean background)

Other ethnic group (17. Arab; 18. Any other ethnic group)[14]

Could it be that because the idea that there are biological races has been successfully dismantled, the ONS has dropped the use of the term "race" for "ethnicity" but then classified ethnicities as belonging to broad racial categories? Or is it some discomfort with the term that led the ONS to drop the term but then continue with racial classifications, just by another name?[15] That doesn't seem quite right, as many of the available options seem straightforwardly ethnic (Indian, Chinese) as opposed to racial, but others are clearly racial (White and Black Caribbean, for example). I won't try to answer these questions here, but there is clearly no sharp distinction between race and ethnicity at work in the UK Census.

The UK Census is used as a basis for various governmental and non-governmental surveys and documents. As in the United States, people are asked to self-identify. There are some exceptions to that, however. For example, Scotland records ethnicity on death certificates, and presumably not on the basis of self-identification, but relies on others to bear witness to the deceased's ethnic identification (Christie 2012).

The conferralist model can be used to illuminate the construction of proper ethnic categories as well, whether institutional or communal. The key idea simply is that social categories are constructed and maintained when a feature of an individual has social significance in a context such that individuals taken to have the feature get conferred onto them a social status in the context.

---

[14] See Classifications at the Office for National Statistics, "Classifications and Harmonisation," accessed May 24, 2017, https://www.ons.gov.uk/methodology/classificationsandstandards.

[15] Compare when people are uncomfortable with using the term "sex" and use "gender" instead, but the answers are *male* or *female*.

5.4 Comparison with Some Other Views on Race

The account of race that I have sketched above is a social constructivist account of race. On this view, being of a certain race is to have a certain social status in a context. This social status can be institutional and consist in rights, privileges, obligations, and other deontic constraints and enablements, or it can be communal and consist in nondeontic constraints on and enablements to a person's behavior in the context.

How does this compare with other accounts of race in the literature? Although it shares in the criticism of biological accounts of race offered by Naomi Zack (1993) and Anthony Appiah (1990, 1996), it is not an eliminativist position. Race exists, it is real, and it is humanly created and sustained, on my view. It shares with Sally Haslanger's position the view that race is a social status, but on Haslanger's view, to be racialized is to have a place in a hierarchical power structure, and the conferralist view does not involve such a claim. My view shares a certain affinity with Charles Mills's position (1998), as he is a constructivist about race. For Mills, social constructivism about race is an objectivist position in that racial categories, and criteria for membership in them, exist independently of any individual subjective attitudes. What determines category membership for Mills is intersubjective agreement on criteria for membership. His is thus a constitutional account, as I have characterized it in this book See Page (59):

> There is intersubjective agreement that having feature B counts as being of race R in context C.

Mills thinks that there is intersubjective agreement that biological ancestry defines race membership in the United States. It is a constructivist position because intersubjective agreement determines the criteria for race membership, as opposed to something subject-independent, such as a mind-independent nature. The difference between my view and Mills's is that mine is a conferralist one, as opposed to a constitutional one, and it is context dependent, whereas Mills aims to give an account of race that works in all situations. On his account, like on Haslanger's, racial classifications are inherently hierarchical. I have not built that in, although when we ask the question why people place each other along racial dimensions, it is hard to ignore the explanation that stigma and privilege attached to different positions in social hierarchies and placings play a role in the enforcement of those hierarchies, with affective attitudes responding to the stigma and the privilege. And it is hard to ignore the further part of such an explanatory story where this enforcement has serious material implications that in turn feed into the stigmatization and privileging of certain people and positions. However, neither the question why we do this nor whether it is justified is a question I address in this book.

What do I mean by saying that race is *real*? The word is used to get at many different distinctions, so let me be clear what I mean by it in this context.

I developed the conferralist framework initially to capture a certain kind of subject dependency of a property. For that reason, in the relevant contexts, when one offers a conferralist account of a feature, one *may* be offering a nonrealist account of it. But that is not the use of "real" in this context. Social properties are dependent on human subjects and their activities in some way. No theorist will deny this. So offering a conferralist story of that dependence is not to offer an antirealist account of the phenomenon.[16] Such a use of "real" does not get at a useful distinction in this context. It does not carve up the pie of views at all, so to speak. One use that does carve up the pie in this particular context is in contrast to the *nominalist*. On a nominalist view such as Ian Hacking's *dynamic nominalism* of human kinds and Ronald Sundstrom's dynamic nominalism of race (2002), racial kinds come into being with the availability of labels or descriptions for them, and don't exist independently of those labels and descriptions. I think social categories and social statuses can exist even though there is no label or description of them yet available. In that sense, my view is *realist*. I also share with other social constructivists the view that races are objective objects of knowledge: we can investigate them through empirical methods. While they are of our own making, they take off leading a life of their own.[17]

5.5 Religion

As I write this in the spring of 2017, in Durham, North Carolina, religious prejudice, among other kinds of prejudice, is on the rise, and sanctioned by the powers that be. Being Muslim, for example, has taken on a social significance that rivals its significance in the aftermath of 9/11. Being Muslim is now a host of contextually dependent social statuses, some institutional,

---

[16] Some theorists seem to read my work that way, for example, Elizabeth Barnes (2016b).

[17] Races and other social categories are also *real* in the other sense that having that conferred status has profound effects on the persons so placed and classified, their life options and material reality. Thanks to Stephanie Kapusta for stressing this point.

other communal. The institutional statuses derive from the various institutions a person may be part of, whether religious, legal, or otherwise, and the base properties are often encoded in laws or regulations. The communal statuses can sometimes "shadow" the institutional ones in the sense that there is an attempt to track what the institutional statuses may be. But sometimes the base properties for the communal status have very little to do with any institutional status—in fact, may not have anything to do with anything actually related to religious or cultural practices of the group in question, but rather may be based in prejudice and propaganda.

Since I maintain that social properties, including institutional and communal ones, are conferred, some historically significant social properties may seem to be counterexamples to that.[18] Being Jewish is a salient one. It may seem that persons are Jewish independently of whether they have that status conferred upon them. For instance, one may hold that, given the authoritative interpretation of Jewish law, one is Jewish if one's mother is Jewish, that is, having a mother of Jewish ancestry constitutes being Jewish. Or one may hold that simply belonging to a community organized around certain cultural and/or religious practices constitutes being Jewish.

This is a complicated case, but the conferralist framework can do it justice. We should keep in mind that the main aim of the account I am offering is to account for socially salient categories and properties, phenomena that *make a social difference*. I think that being Jewish is not one distinct property but a cluster of institutional and communal properties.

Consider the communal property of being Jewish, which is fleshed out in terms of communal constraints and enablements in a communal setting. One is communally Jewish, in a context, if one is taken to have the base property for the conferral of the communal property. On the account I am advancing, there is nothing more to being communally Jewish than functioning as such: if you pass as one in a context, you are one in that context. This is because what it means to have that property in the context is for you to be the subject of constraints and enablements that come with that status in that context. This status is conferred upon you in the context by people with standing in the context.

Consider now the case of the institutional property of being Jewish that is grounded in the heritage of the mother, according to Talmudic law. This is an institutional property because it is codified and has its roots in the authority of Talmudic law. But here a conferralist interpretation of

---

[18] Thanks to Nancy Bauer for this objection.

the situation works just as well. One doesn't function institutionally in the Jewish community, or in the society at large (in those societies where that status comes with institutional privileges and burdens), unless one gets classified as having that status, unless one gets certified, if you will. Institutionally, one is not Jewish if one does not function as Jewish institutionally, if one does not have the privileges and burdens that come with that status.

This may seem counterintuitive. What accounts for the range of reactions to the discovery that a person does or doesn't have the base properties of a particular status? For example, how do we account for the discovery that someone is Jewish during oppressive regimes such as Germany's Third Reich?

Here we must distinguish between meeting the requirements for the conferral of a certain institutional or communal status (having the base properties) and having that status. The institutional status of being Jewish during the Third Reich was introduced with the rise of Nazism and differed in base properties from what had been in practice before. It was, if you will, a new institutional status and accompanied by an ideology whose aim was to justify it. It was related to other older institutional statuses and to some communal statuses in that some of the base properties were the same, but nevertheless it was a new status. Persons did not acquire that status until it was conferred upon them by authorities that judged them to meet the requirements, that is, judged them to have the base properties.

Does this mean that people of Jewish ancestry, who had converted to Catholicism some generations earlier, but who were persecuted during the Third Reich, then effectively became Jewish when certified as Jewish by the Third Reich? No, we need not say that. What we can say is that the Third Reich created a new institutional category of person, *person of Jewish ancestry*, and persecuted members of that category, irrespective of their own self-conception and affiliation. Many of those, of course, were members of Jewish communities, into which they had been initiated in childhood, and continued to engage in practices that kept them in good standing in those communities. They thus had other institutional statuses as Jewish, as conferred onto them by rabbis of their communities. However, the institutional status created by the Nazi authorities was a new one, and people acquired that status by being certified as meeting the requirements by the Nazi authorities.

As with other institutional statuses, whether you meet the requirements for the conferral may become irrelevant down the line, as in the case where you get issued a certificate of some sort and subsequently your institutional status is grounded in the presence of that certificate, not the presence of the base properties at issue in the original conferral. Whether it becomes irrelevant or not depends on the context and depends on whether the certificate is itself a base property in the conferral of the subsequent status or mere evidence of the presence of the base property.

Back to being Jewish. On top of the various institutional properties of being Jewish, there may be contexts in which having the institutional status of being Jewish or of having a certain ethnic, culture, or religious practices, is communally salient and in which being presumed to have any of those features comes with certain communal constraints and enablements that are not institutional. This is one sense in which being Jewish can be socially constructed, as understood in this work.

5.6 Disability

I have mentioned disability as an example in chapter 2, but let me here attend to how I think social categories involving disability get created and sustained. Institutional disability status gets conferred onto people taken to have the base properties for the conferral in each institutional context.[19] For example, an individual with a disability is defined by the Americans with Disabilities Act (ADA) thus:

> a person who has a physical or mental impairment that substantially limits one or more major life activities, a person who has a history or record of such an impairment, or a person who is perceived by others as having such an impairment.[20]

What such a definition does is to put into law what the base properties for the conferral should be. What is striking about this definition is that the base property can not only be a physical or mental impairment that substantially limits one or more major life activities or having a record of such an impairment, but also be "perceived by others to have such an impairment." Having a communal status as a person with disabilities is thus

---

[19] Silvers and Francis (2017) argue that "fundamentally ['disability'] is a term of art, constructed to have different meanings and therefore to apply to different collections of individuals depending on the purpose of the program in which it is used." The conferralist framework offers metaphysical support for such a view.
[20] U.S. Department of Justice, "A Guide to Disability Rights Laws," July 2009, https://www.ada.gov/cguide.htm.

one of the base properties for the conferral of the legal status of being a person with disabilities in the contexts in which the ADA law is in effect.

People can get conferred onto them an institutional status as a person with a disability for certain purposes and not others. For example, a person may have the status of being disabled for the purposes of the ADA antidiscrimination law, but not for the purposes of Social Security disability benefits, as they are not taken to have the base property for the conferral of the latter. The status conferred consists in the deontic constraints on and enablements to their behavior in the institutional context. In this case, it consists in what they can and cannot do in their institutional role.

The communal status of being disabled is also conferred onto people taken to have one of the base properties for the conferral in each context, and it can vary with context what properties serve as the basis for the conferral. Perhaps we can say that physical and mental impairment are the abstract base properties the conferrers are aiming to track, but what features count as evidence of such impairment can vary widely. Also, what significance it has to have a particular feature, if any, can vary widely. In one context, exhibiting certain behaviors can be taken as evidence of artistic expression, in another of mental impairment, in a third of divine communion. Similarly, what in one context is taken as a sign of laziness, can in another be taken as a sign of moral failing, and in a third as a sign of a physical impairment. And what is the upshot of having the status conferred? Communal constraints on and enablements to your behavior in the context. For example, you may be taken to be physically impaired as you limp; such can be the power of the stigma associated with a certain status. At the milonga no one wants to dance with you, even though there is nothing wrong with your tango. Moreover, no one will even talk with you, as if they are afraid to catch your limp. Or, alternatively, having certain impairments can be associated culturally with certain powers or insights, and your limp may be an indication that you possess great wisdom, and people may treat you accordingly.

How does what I say about the social categories of being a person with a disability relate to disputes over what it is to be disabled and recent theories of what disability is? Mine is an account of the feature *having a disability* as a social feature. A person may have other features, for example certain physical characteristics, that serve as base properties for the conferral of the social feature being disabled (institutional or communal). My account is not an account of which properties *should* be the base properties for the conferral of the status; rather it shows that such a conversation needs to take place and that nature does not dictate the matter.

It is helpful to compare my account of disability as a social status with a recent account of disability, offered by Elizabeth Barnes (2016a), where she argues that to be physically disabled is not inherently bad but simply to have a minority body. She also puts forward an account of what it is to be (physically) disabled:

S is physically disabled in context C iff

  (i) S is in some bodily state x
  (ii) The rules for making judgments about solidarity employed by the disability rights movement classify x in context C as among the physical conditions that they are seeking to promote justice for. (46)

On Barnes's account, the disability rights movement determines what *ought* to be the base properties for the status of being disabled in a particular context, and one is disabled in a context just in case one has one of the base features in that context. Hers is not quite a conferralist view, as I characterize it in this book, but rather a constitution account: one is disabled just in case one has the feature in question irrespective of whether one is taken to have it. Which feature? It isn't Searlean collective acceptance that determines that, but rather the disability rights movement.

Her account is an ameliorative one,[21] where we ask, What do we want that category for? Her answer is that we need the category of disability as the basis for solidarity in a political struggle. For that reason, the deciders on what features are relevant are those that are party to that struggle. The people who have the relevant features in a particular context are disabled in that context, irrespective of whether they are recognized as having that feature in the context.

Here is the difference between our proposals, which reflects a difference in the kind of question we are asking.

I ask, What is it to belong to the social category of being disabled in a context (institutional or communal)? Answer: it is to be taken to have a feature that is the basis of the conferral of certain constraints and enablements in the context.

---

[21] Cf. Haslanger 2012.

Barnes asks, What is it to have the feature of being (physically) disabled? Answer: it is to have a physical feature that the disability rights movement decides to promote justice for.

Barnes's proposal, as it is an ameliorative one, can then also answer the normative question that my analysis invites: which base property *should* be the base property for the conferral of a social status of being disabled (institutional or communal)? Her answer is that for the purposes of social justice and solidarity, the base property for the conferral of the status should be the features (in a context) that the disability rights movement decides on as worth fighting for.[22]

5.7 Concluding Remarks

I have discussed some applications of the conferralist framework to actual cases. Readers may disagree with me about some details regarding the conferral of a particular category, even if they agree that the conferralist framework is in general helpful to make sense of it. In particular, they may, for example, disagree about which features serve as the base feature for conferral in institutional or communal contexts. Getting such accounts right requires empirical work that colleagues in related fields are engaged in, fields such as history, sociology, and anthropology, as well as more interdisciplinary fields such as queer theory, critical race theory, trans* theory, disability theory, and religious studies. My main aim here is not to enter into debates about specific details, but rather to outline the structure of such accounts, and I've only provided enough detail so that the reader can project how such accounts would be fleshed out. A different sort of critique would reject altogether this framework for makings sense of social categories, or, more narrowly, to reject the framework for a particular category.

---

[22] There is room for error here, as the leadership of the disability rights movement can be wrong about which features should be the base features for the conferral because it is applying their own solidarity standards inconsistently or unfairly. But there is no further authority about what the solidarity standards should be.

CHAPTER 6 | Identity as Social Location

6.1 Introduction

The focus of this book has been on how to account for the nature of social categories of individuals, how they are created and maintained. And the story has almost exclusively focused on what people do *to* each other: how they classify and place each other in the various contexts in which they find themselves. But what about our own roles in our own predicaments? And what about our thoughts, feelings, attitudes, and self-conceptions? What roles do they play?

In order to answer those questions, we need to turn our focus to the notion of *identity*. I want to articulate a conception of *social* identity that complements the conception of social categories set forth in this book.

Recall the reflections of Rebecca Solnit and Guillermo Gómez-Peña as they travel through San Francisco that I mentioned earlier. Solnit experiences herself as Western in Chinatown, as white in Bayview, as straight and female in the Castro. Gómez-Peña is mistaken for a tourist from Argentina in Chinatown, at the Bollywood Café he is "the wrong kind of brown", in the Castro he is an older gay man, and in the financial district he is nobody. The fact that Solnit and Gómez-Peña *experience* themselves in these diverse ways as they travel through the city illustrates well some of the complexity of identity. It brings into focus not only how different features of ourselves are socially salient in different contexts, but also how we sometimes are acutely aware of how others see us and place us. My intention in this chapter is to articulate a conception of social identity that does justice to those experiences and meets certain other substantive constraints, which are generated by our wish for an account of identity in the first place. The result will be a more complex and nuanced story of our social interactions and our role in the creation and maintenance of *communal* social categories in particular.

6.2 What Do We Want a Theory of Social Identity For?

In the broadest possible terms, we want a theory of identity that can help us understand why people do what they do. Of course, a theory of identity is not going to accomplish that all by its lonesome, but is rather an important piece in a big puzzle which is a theory of practical rationality and agency.

What is the relationship between a theory of identity and a theory of *social* identity, and how do we decide what considerations are relevant to each? I think here we do well to focus on the various features we have. We all have a myriad of features, but only some of them help form our identities. Can we say anything in general about the features that do?

Amélie Rorty and David Wong (1993) think that identity in general is constituted by a configuration of central traits that make a systematic difference to a person's life. What makes a trait central on their view? They distinguish a variety of ways in which a trait can be central and think of its centrality as a matter of degree (1993: 19):

Objective ramification: the degree to which other traits depend on the trait

Contextual ramification: the degree to which a trait is exemplified across many and diverse contexts

Resistance to change: the degree to which it is difficult to change the trait

Social ramification: the degree to which it affects the way persons are categorized and treated by others

Dominance in conflict: the extent to which it is dominant in contexts that require coping with stress of conflict

Trump factor: to what extent it trumps when it conflicts with other traits

Importance to self-conception: to what extent persons would regard themselves as radically changed were they to lose the trait

Rorty and Wong's characterization can help us isolate those features that play a role in the formation of our social identities: they are the features whose presence has *social ramifications*. And drawing on our discussion of the construction of social categories in the book so far, the features that play a role in constituting our *social identity* are the various features that serve as the basis for the conferral of a social status in a context.

As I see it, when we seek an account of social identity, we seek a theoretical framework that can help us understand certain constraints on and enablements to people's lives and life options that are not direct consequences of their physical or mental characteristics, talents, inclinations, or mere legal status, but that rather arise from the fact that the various features they have matter socially in a context. These constraints I have in mind can be imposed by others, and by the people themselves. Not only do we want to make sense of identity-based oppression, although that is certainly part of the goal, but also to make sense of the limiting or enabling of life options that need not be pernicious. The account thus needs to integrate a metaphysical picture of the mechanics of identity and identity formation with a plausible picture of the subject as an agent, whose actions not only contribute to the formation of identity, but for whom identity is also a source of reason for action.

Given this larger goal of offering an account of identity, here are the constraints the account has to meet:

1. Do justice to how our identity is constrained by others.
2. Do justice to our own contribution to our identity.
3. Do justice to how highly contextual our identity is.
4. Make sense of the phenomenon of passing.
5. Make sense of the intersection of the various aspects of our identity.
6. Be compatible with a plausible account of agency in which identity can be a source of reason for action, including a moral reason for action.

6.3 Why These Constraints?

These constraints represent assumptions and theoretical commitments. Not everyone will share all of them, but by making them explicit, we can at least have a discussion about which of these assumptions and commitments to hold on to. It is, for instance, an assumption that I make that our subjective identity, in terms of which we see ourselves and which guides our conscious agency, is deeply social in the sense that the categories available for us for forming our self-conception depend on the social contexts we live in. Our subjective self-conception thus depends on the socially available categories, and our subjective identity is therefore constrained by others in a way that the account has to spell out. But having an identity also requires a commitment on our part. Our identity is not simply given to us by others; we have to embrace it as our own.

That our identity is highly *contextual* has been explored by many feminist theorists. María Lugones (1987:3) famously speaks of "world-traveling" and how she is viewed and treated differently in different contexts and the effects it has on her. I want the account of identity to capture that contextuality.

Making sense of *passing* is something that an account like mine has to address specifically, given the account of social properties it rests on. For on the account of social properties I offer, a person has the social property just in case she is taken to have the base property for the conferral of the social property. On a superficial reading of that, someone is a woman simply if she passes as a woman. But how can we then make sense of the intuitive difference between being a woman and passing as a woman? This is a worry my account will have to address. Moreover, the phenomenon of passing is an important issue in its own right that raises questions of justice and morality, as well as metaphysics, and any account of identity needs to address it.

Making sense of how the various aspects of our identity intersect is important to address given the charge by Kimberle Crenshaw (1989, 1991) and others that an additive model of identity—in which you analyze the various axes of oppression separately (being a woman, being African American, being lesbian, being a single mother, etc.) and then simply add them up—doesn't do justice to the oppression people in that complex social location find themselves. As is well known, Crenshaw has pushed for an intersectional analysis to capture the experiences of being a black woman, for example, that is over and above the experiences of *being black + being a woman*. I want the account I offer to involve the assumption that our identity is not a simple aggregate of its various parts, and in that way it will do justice to the *intersectionalist* assumption.

That identity can be a source of reason for action should not be controversial, but whether that reason can be a moral one could be. I will, however, say very little about that constraint and what a plausible account of human agency in which identity can be a moral reason for action looks like. I hope to address that at a later date. But it is a constraint on the account of social identity that it be compatible with an account of agency in which social identity can be a source of a reason for action, including a moral one.

6.4 The Metaphor of Identity as Social Location

Although "social location" sometimes refers to class status exclusively, it has become commonplace to use the term to refer to a person's place in a system of social relations more generally, where the social relations in question need not involve social or economic class exclusively. It is the location metaphor that I want to explore. This metaphor works on a number of levels. On a descriptive level, the metaphor captures how we try to make sense of our relationships to other people, by drawing a picture of a social landscape and locating ourselves in that picture. It also captures our attempt to make sense of other people and their behavior by placing them in categories that serve as explanatory of their behavior, and which are to justify our treatment of them.

I want to flesh out this metaphor by weaving together my account of the construction of social categories with an account of the role of the subjects themselves in a way that meets the constraints I've mentioned.

6.5 Identity in Context

Let's go back to Rebecca Solnit and Guillermo Gómez-Peña in *Infinite City* and attempt to articulate a more nuanced story of the social mechanics at work. We can assume that the physical features Solnit and Gómez-Peña have remain constant. What varies, though, is which of those features are intelligible and which are socially salient. In some contexts, they are even taken to have some features they don't have. The salient features set the constraints on what roles they can have in the context, and the roles they have constrain their actions as well as enable some actions.

Let me appeal to the metaphor of a game to spell out the details of this idea of a feature or property being "intelligible" and its being "socially salient." Consider a game and its rules. Consider chess, for example. The rules of chess determine which bodily movements count as moves in the game. There are certain bodily movements that count as moves, and others that count as breaking the rules. Still others don't count at all; those movements don't even register; they are unintelligible.

For instance, scratching your ear while you think will not register, whereas moving a piece from one place on the board to another may count as a move in the game, or it might be inadmissible and call for a negative reaction such as "no, you can't do that!" from your partner. Generally speaking, bodily movements during a game of chess are of three types:

(1) movements that count as moves in the game; (2) movements that register but don't count as admissible moves in the game; (3) movements that don't register at all, are not intelligible.

The *constitutive* rules of chess are rules of admissibility and intelligibility within the game. The rules of admissibility don't set the standards for what is a good or bad move, although we are likely to want to give an account of what the standards of good and bad chess moves are that makes it a function of the rules and the arrangement of pieces at a particular time.

Let's linger on the distinction among constitutive rules, regulative rules, and norms.[1] Constitutive rules are the rules that give meaning to a certain behavior or feature in a particular context and, in that way, bring new phenomena into being. For example, "when a batter has had three strikes, he is out" gives meaning to the phenomenon of a batter's having three strikes and specifies the consequences of that. The batter can no longer take a pitch and has to leave the field. Then, depending on the score of the game, the next batter steps up or the other team gets a go, provided we are not at the end of the game. If we flout a constitutive rule, then we are no longer playing the game; we have ceased to engage in that activity.

Regulative rules regulate behavior that is already going on. For instance, the rule *you must drive on the right side on the road* regulates driving activity that would be utter chaos if unregulated, but it does not give meaning to the behavior that results in a different status or entity. If we flout this rule, it's not the case that we are no longer driving. We are still engaging in the activity, but we might be subject to sanctions of some sort. Compare with the rule: *if you drive on the wrong side of the road, that is a traffic violation*. This rule gives meaning to the activity of driving against traffic and specifies that doing so constitutes violating traffic laws. If you flout a rule like *to drive legally, you must drive on the right side of the road*, you have ceased to engage in the activity *legal driving*, and have started doing something else (driving illegally).

Norms are what our behavior is evaluated under, by others and by ourselves. Norms of good chess playing, for example, are the standards we should adhere to if we want to play the game of chess *well*. We can flout these norms and people may make fun of our playing or show us other forms of disrespect, but we are still playing chess, albeit badly. And, of course, our adherence to such norms is not simply on or off, but comes in degrees: I may play really well for the first part of the match, but then tire and make a stupid mistake. The hold norms have on us and the extent to

---

[1] For the distinction between constitutive and regulative rules, see Searle 1969.

which we try to regulate our own behavior in reference to them similarly come in degrees. I may dress in a way that accords with the standards of femininity in a particular context, but my outspokenness and body language may not accord with how a woman should behave.[2]

Going back to chess, salient bodily movements are those that count as admissible moves in the game, or those that count as inadmissible. The unintelligible movements are the ones that don't count as either admissible or inadmissible.

I want to make use of this discussion of *intelligibility* and *saliency* in two ways. First, in different contexts, different features of people are going to be intelligible and a subset of those are going to be socially salient or meaningful. The socially salient ones are the ones that are the base features for the conferral of a certain social property in the context; the conferral of a social status involves constraints and enablements. The socially meaningful features serve as the base features in *placings*.

As we discussed earlier, some properties can be socially salient in one context but not in another. For instance, there are contexts in which having red hair is intelligible, but not socially salient. And there have been contexts in which having red hair has been socially salient and grounds for discrimination and harassment.

But, as I made clear before, it isn't the actual presence of the salient property that matters, but whether a person is taken to have the property that grounds the conferral. So the main idea is that a person is taken to have a certain property, and if that property is salient in that context, that helps set the boundaries of what he or she can do and not do in that context. The perception that the property is present places the person in one of the recognizable social categories in that context.

A similar story can be said about behavior as about properties. We can think of a person's exhibiting a certain behavior as (logically) on par with having a feature: A is F.

While the game metaphor can help us make sense of the idea that a property or behavior is intelligible or socially meaningful in a context, it breaks down in important ways, especially when applied to behavior in a context.

If the game metaphor worked perfectly, then the social rules in a context would be explicit, and particular behavior in a context would count as a move in a social game (if admissible), as flouting the rules (if inadmissible),

---

[2] It may be more accurate to say that gender norms have many dimensions and that adherence to these norms along each dimension comes in degrees. That would help explain the apparent conflict in the example here.

or as behavior that was intelligible but did not contribute to the game (if neither, yet registered). But several features of the social context distinguish it from the chess game. The rules are not explicit, and they are not simply constitutive rules but a mixture of constitutive rules and regulative rules or regulative norms. These norms may be such that the people who are responsive to them and judged in accordance with them may not be able to articulate them and may not even be conscious of them. Worse still, which norms apply in the context isn't hard and fast, but is negotiated in the context. How exactly? It is here that we turn to the metaphor of identity as social location and the placing of ourselves and each other on a map of those locations. There are several things that get negotiated in a context: what roles there are to play, who plays what role, and what the expectations are of each role.

6.6 The Hegelian Model

I think that what roles there are to play in a context can be captured by an overlapping consensus of social maps the participants in a context are working with. These social maps need not be known consciously. Most often they are unconscious. I think we can turn to Hegel's account of subjectification and objectification (1807) to make sense of the negotiation that takes place over which social map is operating in the context. We will have to complicate the picture a bit, but the dynamics are similar.

You will remember that on Hegel's account, consciousness forms a conception of itself and acts out this conception, which is to say, acts as if that conception is true of it. Consciousness also forms a conception of the other and acts as if that conception is true of it. In the case when the other is another consciousness, both consciousnesses form conceptions of themselves and the other and attempt to act out these conceptions, act as if they were true. Hegel, of course, describes a dramatic battle of wills in the master/slave dialectic: these two consciousnesses battle over whose self-conception and conception of the other is to prevail. This battle is to the brink of death, at which point one of them values life more than its self-conception and conception of the other and gives in.

6.7 The Hegel-Inspired Social Map Model

We don't have to go so far as to talk of "masters" and "slaves" and battles to the death to make use of Hegel's insight into how negotiation over whose conception of the social space and the roles in it prevails. Participants in a context bring to it their own map of social relations and place themselves and the other participants on the map, consciously or subconsciously. They then act as if their map and their placement on the map is correct. The overlapping map consensus sets the starting point for negotiation of the roles people can play in a context.

It is probably more accurate to say that people bring a set of maps with them to the encounter and "choose", however unconsciously, one that seems to them best to fit, given the characteristics the participants seem to have.

So the suggestion for how to unpack the metaphor of identity as social location is this: The identity we have in a particular context is the result of an ongoing negotiation over which social map is operative in the context and where on the social map the various participants in the context are. This social map is a cognitive map that sets the conditions for intelligibility for behavior in the context and sets the parameters for admissible behavior. It also enables behavior. The map is the representation of our social landscape, of course. Our identity is the location in that landscape.

We are drawing on the Hegelian picture, but complicating it a bit. It is not just two consciousnesses that bring conceptions of themselves and of each other to a meeting; rather, there can be many. And instead of bringing these conceptions, they bring a map of the available categories and criteria for membership in each. None of this need be conscious.

What is it then to have an identity on the account offered? Our *objective social identity* is simply the location on a social map that we occupy stably, with its associated norms of behavior. We can have an objective social identity without being aware that we do. When we are aware of our location, we can react to it by acting in accordance with the corresponding norms or by resisting them. However, if we do identify with the location we inhabit stably, then, if we act in accordance with the norms of that location, we can come to fit our location ever better. There is thus a certain "looping-effect" possible, much discussed in the literature (Hacking 1999).

Our *subjective social identity* is the location on the social map in the context that we identify with. The location consists in constraints on and enablements to one's behavior, and accompanying it are social norms for behavior befitting that social location. We are evaluated with respect to these norms by other people, and when we identify with the location, we take these norms as applying to us and behave always in reference to them, even when we are resisting them. In Charlotte Witt's words (2011: 32–33), we are "responsive to and evaluable under" these norms.

Our subjective social identity can be the location we inhabit stably, but it need not be. It may be a location on a social map that most contexts don't allow us to inhabit. Sometimes there is no location in the current context that we identify with. And sometimes there are very few contexts with locations that we identify with. Our struggle then is to make it the case that there are more contexts in which there are locations that we can identify with.

6.8 How the Account Meets the Constraints

It should be clear from what I have said how identity is constrained by others on this picture, and also how we ourselves contribute to our own identity. Similarly, since I have highlighted that identity rests on what features we are perceived to have in a context and which of those are socially salient in that context, it should be clear that the picture of identity painted here makes it out to be highly contextual.

But I have yet to touch upon the other constraints on the account I explicitly listed: passing and intersectionality. I will not say anything about how the account fits with a plausible account of agency here, but let me turn to the other two issues now.

6.8.1 Passing

There is a worry about social constructionist accounts of phenomena such as identity that they cannot makes sense of passing (Mallon 2004, 2016). Why would this be a worry for social constructionist accounts, and would my account be subject to it? The worry rests on the idea that, to be able to make sense of the phenomenon of passing, that is, when a person passes for a member of K for some K ("passes for K" for short), the account needs to make a distinction between really being K and being perceived as being K. Social constructionist accounts share the feature that the epistemic partly determines the metaphysical—the details on that vary, of course. But in this case, being perceived to have the base property for a particular identity in a context confers that identity onto the person in such a way that the person has to negotiate that and either trouble the conferral or accept it and act in accordance with it. How do we make sense of the idea that a person passes as K if we think that being K just is to be perceived as K, or something close to that?

The answer is that this is not a precise description of what goes on. I say that the property of being a woman, say, gets conferred on a person in a context if that person is perceived to have the base property (or a sufficient number of base properties). And this is enough to make sense of passing:

> A person passes as having the base property for the conferral of the status woman, when they don't have the property and the knowledge of that lack would result in the revoking of the status. The person is a woman in that context, but passes as having the base feature.

So while I cannot draw a meaningful distinction between passing as a woman in a context and being a woman in a context, I can make sense of the phenomenon of misidentification and the various emotional responses to the discovery that misidentification took place. The misidentification concerns the presence of the base properties, however.

6.8.2 Intersectionality

There has been considerable discussion for a couple of decades now over the adequacy of giving accounts of a particular social identity in the absence of the other identities people inhabit. In this way, it has been argued that we cannot give an account of what it is to be a woman, say, without taking into account the other social categories she occupies, such as her race, sexuality, class, and the like.

There is a version of the demand for intersectional theorizing that threatens the possibility of theorizing about identity altogether. For if the demand is that we take into account all dimensions of the person, don't we encounter one of two problems: that it is an impossible task because of the number of dimensions or, if we manage to give such an account, that it has ceased to have any force because there are no general lessons we can draw from an account of the singular identity of a particular person?

I don't think we find ourselves in this predicament for the simple reason that each context determines which base properties are salient in the context, and the corresponding identities can be very fine-grained. We can have white men, black men, white women, and black women in one context, and much more fine-grained identities in another, such as mixed-race trans* people, white trans* people, black trans* people, native trans* people, cis people, and so on.

The constraints and enablements one has in a particular context are complicated products of the constraints and enablements that the significance of each feature brings. It is not simply additive, because presence of some features can trump that of others.

6.9 Social Identity and Social Categories

It is a virtue of the account of identity that I have offered that it can accommodate the intesectionalist assumption. But now a worry arises.[3] Do we want to say that, say, black women are a separate social category and distinct from black and from women? And if so, what of black wiccan lesbian women? Is that also a separate social category? If we accept that it is, then it seems we have a proliferation of social categories, as fine-grained as one wants. Not only is the metaphysics then exceedingly messy; it is also not clear how we are to account for the solidarity among the many individuals who share some features and are oppressed on the basis of that.

To answer that worry, let me remind the reader that social categories get formed and maintained through the individual actions of classifying and placing. To be of a category, say, to be a woman, is to have a certain status in a context on the basis of being taken to have some feature. There is no context-independent feature. They also change over time. In the future, there may be different social categories, both institutional and communal ones, some of which are what we would now consider intersectional.

Crenshaw's original focus in urging that we employ an intersectional analysis was on the function of antidiscrimination law and how it was impossible to capture legally certain burdens that black women faced if we only were able to explore whether they had suffered discrimination *as Black* or *as women*. With such blunt tools, the mistreatment was not visible.

The general story is that we have features, and some of those features have social significance in a context, and the status we enjoy in a particular context is the result of the constraints and enablements that the presence of each and every one of our socially significant features brings, where the presence of some features can trump others. Legal categories, on the other hand, typically don't include such intersectional statuses, and in order to combat certain kinds of discrimination, it may be necessary to introduce such intersectional legal categories.

---

[3] Thanks to Cat Saint-Croix for this worry.

6.10 Final Words

My motivation for articulating an account of identity was to attend more closely to the mechanics of how people come to have the social properties they have. I had already given an account of what it was to have these social properties, but the precise mechanism of how we acquired them was still a bit of a mystery. Attending to the subjective and objective aspects of identity in a context is an important piece in that puzzle. But giving an account of identity is also an important part of giving an account of agency and of giving an account of certain kinds of oppression. And it has been my contention here that the conception of identity expressed in the metaphor of identity as a social location is rich enough to do the work we want it to do.

CONCLUSION | Categories We Live By
          | *Systematicity and Oppression*

WHAT I HAVE OFFERED in this book is an answer to the questions, What is a social category? What is its nature? How is it created and sustained? My answer is that individual agents create and maintain social categories by the conferral actions of *classifying* and *placing* people in the contexts they travel.

One of the motivations for giving an account of social categories is to give us tools to think about oppressive institutions and practices, and it may seem that such a radically context-dependent account of social categories may not be up to the task. It will only be helpful if it can help us explain some systematic aspects of phenomena such as gender oppression and ground our claims to solidarity with people in faraway places and times. Can this account do that?

Let me in conclusion address how the account offered can explain the systematicity of phenomena such as gender oppression and make claims about social categories across contexts.

Consider the communal feature of being a woman, for example. On the view advocated in this book, there is no answer to the question, Are you really a woman? There is no *real* way of being a woman, and there is no being a woman *simpliciter*. Being a woman is a social status to be had in a context, and one may have it in some contexts and not others. And, as mentioned before, the fact that one does or does not have the status in a particular context does not mean that one ought or ought not have that status. A separate normative argument is needed for such a claim.

But here is the worry: on what grounds can we say that there is anything that the various people in the various contexts share? How can we ground the insight that there is a systematic mistreatment of women going on around the world?

Since no one is a woman plain and simple, but only a woman relative to a context, there are two things that can ground our claims that there is something systematic going on: we can point to shared base properties, and we can point to similarities in constraints and enablements.

When we focus on the fact that having certain features, such as certain body parts, sex assignment, skin color, or ancestry serves as the basis for the conferral of a social status in many contexts, we see that there is differential treatment on the basis of these features in many different parts of the world. We can thus draw general conclusions on the basis of how widespread differential treatment on the basis of these features is. And as people come to each new encounter with the social maps that have operated in their prior contexts, we can get a picture of the systematicity of certain sorts of differential treatment in a way that still preserves the dynamic nature of human interaction and does not posit structures or structural agency. The creators and maintainers of our institutions and practices are individual human agents.

The other sort of observation of systematicity we can make is in the constraints and enablements that come with a certain social status. We can, for example, observe that similar constraints and enablements are present across a range of contexts, even though the base properties (and accompanying ideologies) may differ.

But how are we to ground claims to solidarity across space and time? Can we say that there were gays in ancient Greece? We can ground such claims to solidarity on the basis of the fact that certain features that serve as the base properties for the conferral of the status of being gay in twenty-first-century San Francisco or Sidney were also present in ancient Greece, even though the constraints and enablements that came with the conferred status (if there were any) were different from the contemporary ones.

We are similarly able to ground our claim to solidarity with women in contexts near and far in time and space without insisting that to be a woman is to have the base features in question. We can meet the theoretical demand for the answer to the "woman question" in feminist theory[1] while at the same time rejecting the question, and thus avoiding the problem of exclusion that has plagued substantive answers to that question.

---

[1] Cf. Moi 1999; Alcoff 2006; Haslanger 2012; Mikkola 2016.

BIBLIOGRAPHY

Alcoff, Linda Martín. 2006. *Visible Identities: Race, Gender, and the Self.* New York: Oxford University Press.

Andreasen, Robin. 2000. "Race: Biological Reality of Social Construct?" *Philosophy of Social Science* 67, no. 3: 666.

Anscombe, G. E. M. (1957) 1963. *Intention.* 2nd ed. Oxford: Basil Blackwell.

Appiah, Kwame Anthony. 1990. "Racisms." In *Anatomy of Racism*, edited by David Theo Goldberg, 3–17. Minneapolis: University of Minnesota Press.

———. 1996. "Race, Culture, Identity: Misunderstood Connections." In *Color Conscious: The Political Morality of Race*, edited by Kwame Anthony Appiah and Amy Gutmann, 30–105. Princeton, NJ: Princeton University Press.

Ásta Sveinsdóttir. 2008. "Essentiality Conferred." *Philosophical Studies* 140, no. 1 (July 2008): 135–148.

———. 2011. "The Metaphysics of Sex and Gender." In *Feminist Metaphysics*, edited by Charlotte Witt, 47–65. Dordrecht: Springer.

———. 2012. "Review of *The Metaphysics of Gender*," by Charlotte Witt. *Notre Dame Philosophical Reviews*, May 2012. http://ndpr.nd.edu/news/30682-the-metaphysics-of-gender/.

———. 2013. "The Social Construction of Human Kinds." *Hypatia* 28, no. 4: 716–732.

———. 2015. "Social Construction." *Philosophy Compass* 10, no. 12: 1–9.

Austin, J. L. 1975. *How to Do Things with Words.* 2nd ed. Edited by J. O. Urmson and Marina Sbisà. Cambridge, MA: Harvard University Press.

Bach, Theodore. 2012. "Gender Is a Natural Kind with a Historical Essence." *Ethics* 122, no. 2: 231–272.

Barnes, Elizabeth. 2016a. *The Minority Body: A Theory of Disability.* New York: Oxford University Press

———. 2016b. "Realism and Social Structure." *Philosophical Studies* 174, no. 10: 2417–2433.

Barnes, Mo. 2015. "Rachel Dolezal's Brother Blames Howard University for Her Racial Self-Hatred." *Rollingout*, June 14. http://rollingout.com/2015/06/14/rachel-dolezals-brother-blames-howard-university-to-blame/.

Bauer, Nancy. 2001. *Simone de Beauvoir, Philosophy, and Feminism*. New York: Columbia University Press, 2001

Beauvoir, Simone de. 1949. *Le Deuxième Sexe*. Paris: Librairie Gallimard.

———. *The Second Sex*. 1953. Translated and edited by H. M. Parshley. New York: Alfred A. Knopf.

———. *The Second Sex*. 2010. Translated by Constance Borde and Sheila Malovany-Chevallier. New York: Alfred Knopf.

Bettcher, Talia Mae. 2013. "Trans Women and the Meaning of 'Woman'." In Philosophy of Sex: Contemporary Readings, Sixth Edition, edited by A. Soble, N. Power and R. Halwani, 233–250. Lanman, MD: Rowman & Littlefield.

Blackburn, Simon. 1981. "Rule Following and Moral Realism." In *Wittgenstein: To Follow a Rule*, edited by Steven Holtzman and Christopher Leich, 163–187. London: Routledge and Kegan Paul.

———. 1984. *Spreading the Word*. Oxford: Clarendon Press.

Boghossian, Paul. 2006. *Fear of Knowledge*. Oxford: Oxford University Press.

Boyd, Richard. 1999. "Homeostasis, Species, and Higher Taxa." In *Species: New Interdisciplinary Essays*, edited by Robert A. Wilson, 141–186. Cambridge, MA: MIT Press.

Butler, Judith. 1990. *Gender Trouble: Feminism and the Subversion of Identity*. New York: Routledge.

———. 1992. "Contingent Foundations." In *Feminists Theorize the Political*, edited by J. Butler and J. W. Scott, pp. 3–21. New York: Routledge.

———. 1993. *Bodies that Matter*. New York and London: Routledge.

———. 1997. *Excitable Speech: A Politics of the Performative*. London: Routledge.

Callahan, Gerald. 2009. *Between XX and XY: Intersexuality and the Myth of the Two Sexes*. Chicago: Chicago Review Press.

Christie, Bryan. 2012. "Scotland Introduces Record of Ethnicity on Death Certificates." *The British Medical Journal (BMJ)* 344: e475.

Crenshaw, Kimberle. 1989. "Demarginalizing the Intersection of Race and Sex: A Black Feminist Critique of Antidiscrimination Doctrine, Feminist Theory and Antiracist Politics." *University of Chicago Legal Forum* 140:139–167.

———. 1991. "Mapping the Margins: Intersectionality, Identity Politics, and Violence against Women of Color." *Stanford Law Review* 43, no. 6: 1241–1299.

Davis, F. James. 2001. *Who Is Black?* 20th anniv. ed. Philadelphia: University of Pennsylvania Press.

Dembroff, Robin. 2016. "Oppressive Truths." Unpublished manuscript.

Díaz-León, Esa. 2013. "What Is Social Construction?" *The European Journal of Philosophy* 23, no. 4: 1137–1152.

Elgin, Catherine Z. 1996. *Considered Judgment*. Princeton, NJ: Princeton University Press.

Epstein, Brian. 2015. *The Ant Trap: Rebuilding the Foundations of the Social Sciences*. New York: Oxford University Press.

Fausto-Sterling, Anne. 2000a. "The Five Sexes, Revisited." *The Sciences*, 40: 18–23.

———. 2000b. *Sexing the Body*. New York: Basic Books, 2000.

Fricker, Miranda. 2007. *Epistemic Injustice: The Power and Ethics of Knowing*. Oxford: Oxford University Press.

Glasgow, Joshua. 2008. *A Theory of Race*. New York: Routledge.

Gooding-Williams, Robert. 1988. "Race, Multiculturalism and Democracy." *Constellations* 5: 18–41.

Gould, Stephen Jay. 2000. *The Lying Stones of Marrakech*. New York: Harmony Books.

Habermas, Jürgen. 1986. "Taking Aim at the Heart of the Present." In *Foucault: A Critical Reader*, edited by David Hoy, 103–108. Oxford: Basil Blackwell.

Hacking, Ian. 1990. "Two Kinds of 'New Historicism' for Philosophers." *New Literary History* 21, no. 2: 343–364.

———. 1999. *The Social Construction of What?* Cambridge, MA: Harvard University Press.

———. 2002. *Historical Ontology*. Cambridge, MA: Harvard University Press.

Hardimon, Michael O. 2003. "The Ordinary Concept of Race." *The Journal of Philosophy* 100, no. 9: 437–455.

Haslanger, Sally. 2000. "Gender and Race: (What) Are They? (What) Do We Want Them To Be?" *Noûs* 34, no. 1 (March): 31–55.

———. 2003. "Social Construction: The 'Debunking' Project." In *Socializing Metaphysics*, edited by Frederick Schmitt, 301–325. Lanham, MD: Rowman and Littlefield.

———. 2005. "What Are We Talking About? The Semantics and Politics of Social Kinds." *Hypatia* 20, no. 4: 10–26.

———. 2012. *Resisting Reality: Social Construction and Social Critique*. Oxford: Oxford University Press.

Haslanger, Sally, and Ásta. 2017. "Feminist Metaphysics." In *The Stanford Encyclopedia of Philosophy* (Fall 2017 Edition), edited by Edward N. Zalta https://plato.stanford.edu/archives/fall2017/entries/feminism-metaphysics/.

Hegel, G. W. F. 1807. *Phänomenologie des Geistes*. Bamberg: Joseph Anton Goebhardt.

James, Michael. 2011. "Race." In *The Stanford Encyclopedia of Philosophy* (Spring 2017 Edition), edited by Edward N. Zalta https://plato.stanford.edu/archives/spr2017/entries/race/.

Jenkins, Katharine. 2016. "Amelioration and Inclusion: Gender Identity and the Concept of Woman." *Ethics* 126, no. 2: 394–421.

Johnston, Mark. 1989. "Dispositional Theories of Value." *Proceedings of the Aristotelian Society Supplement*. 63(Suppl): 139–174.

———. 1993. "Objectivity Refigured: Pragmatism without Verificationism." In *Reality, Representation, and Projection*, edited by J. Haldane and C. Wright, 85–130. Oxford: Oxford University Press.

Khalidi, Mohammad Ali. 2013 "Three Kinds of Social Kinds," *Philosophy and Phenomenological Research* 90 (2015): 96–112.

Krisnamurti, Meena. 2017. "Race Talk and Self-Respect: A Philosophical Analysis of the Dolezal Case." *Huffington Post*, March 30. https://www.huffingtonpost.com/entry/race-talk-and-self-respect-a-philosophical-analysis_us_58dce690e4b0efcf4c66a60e.

Langton, Rae. 2009. *Sexual Solipsism: Philosophical Essays on Pornography and Objectification*. New York: Oxford University Press.

———. 2015. "Locke Lectures." Delivered at Oxford.

Lewis, David. 1989. "Dispositional Theories of Value." *Proceedings of the Aristotelian Society Supplement*. 63(Suppl): 113–137.

Ludwig, Kirk. 2014. "Proxy Agency in Collective Action." *Noûs* 48, no. 1: 75–105.

Lugones, María. 1987. "Playfulness, 'World'-Traveling and Loving Perception." *Hypatia* 2, no. 2: 3–19.

Lugones, María, and Elizabeth Spelman. 1983. "Have We Got a Theory for You! Feminist Theory, Cultural Imperialism and the Demand for 'the Woman's Voice.'" *Women's Studies International Forum* 6, no. 6: 573–581.

Maitra, Ishani. 2004. "Silence and Responsibility." *Philosophical Perspectives* 18, no. 1: 189–208.

———. 2009. "Silencing Speech." *Canadian Journal of Philosophy* 39, no. 2 (June): 309–338.

Mallon, Ron. 2003. "Social Construction, Social Roles and Stability." In *Socializing Metaphysics*, edited by F. Schmitt, 327–353. Lanham, MD: Rowman and Littlefield.

———. 2004. "Passing, Traveling, and Reality: Social Construction and the Metaphysics of Race." *Noûs* 38, no. 4: 644–673.

———. 2006. "A Field Guide to Social Construction." *Philosophy Compass* 2, no. 1: 93–108.

———. (2008) 2013. "Naturalistic Approaches to Social Construction." In *The Stanford Encyclopedia of Philosophy* (Winter 2014 Edition), edited by Edward N. Zalta https://plato.stanford.edu/archives/win2014/entries/social-construction-naturalistic/.

———. 2016. *The Construction of Human Kinds*. New York: Oxford University Press.

McDowell, John. 1983. "Aesthetic Value, Objectivity, and the Fabric of the World." In *Pleasure, Preference, and Value*, edited by Eva Schaper, 1–16. Cambridge: Cambridge University Press.

———. 1985. "Values and Secondary Qualities." In *Morality and Objectivity*, edited by Ted Honderich, 110–129. London: Routledge and Kegan Paul.

McGowan, Mary Kate. 2004. "Conversational Exercitives: Something Else We Do with Our Words." *Linguistics and Philosophy* 27, no. 1: 93–111.

———. 2009. "Oppressive Speech." *Australasian Journal of Philosophy* 87, no. 3: 389–407.

McKitrick, Jennifer. 2015. "A Dispositional Account of Gender." *Philosophical Studies* 172, no. 10: 2575–2589.

Mikkola, Mari. 2006. "Elizabeth Spelman, Gender Realism, and Women." *Hypatia* 21, no. 4: 79–96.

———. (2008) 2016. "Feminist Perspectives on Sex and Gender." *The Stanford Encyclopedia of Philosophy* (Winter 2017 Edition), Edward N. Zalta (ed.), URL = <https://plato.stanford.edu/archives/win2017/entries/feminism-gender/>

———. 2011. "Ontological Commitments, Sex and Gender." In *Feminist Metaphysics*, edited by Charlotte Witt, 67–83. Dortrecht: Springer.

Mills, Charles. 1998. *Blackness Visible: Essays on Philosophy and Race*. Ithaca, NY: Cornell University Press.

Mitford, Nancy. 1956. *Nobless Oblige: An Enquiry into the Identifiable Characteristics of the English Aristocracy*. New York: Harper and Brothers Publishers.

Moi, Toril. 1999. *What Is a Woman? And Other Essays*. Oxford: Oxford University Press.

"Norrie May-Welby.2017." Wikipedia. https://en.wikipedia.org/wiki/Norrie_May-Welby.

Oluo, Ijeoma. 2017. "The Heart of Whiteness: Ijeoma Oluo Interviews Rachel Dolezal, the White Woman Who Identifies as Black." *Stranger*, April 19. http://www.thestranger.com/features/2017/04/19/25082450/the-heart-of-whiteness-ijeoma-oluo-interviews-rachel-dolezal-the-white-woman-who-identifies-as-black.

Omi, Michael, and Howard Winant. 1994. *Racial Formation in the United States: From the 1960s to the 1990s*. 2nd ed. New York: Routledge.

Pettit, Philip. 1991. "Realism and Response-Dependence." *Mind* 100, no. 4: 587–626.

Piper, Adrian. 1992. "Passing for White, Passing for Black." *Transition* 58: 4–32.

Plato. 1578. *Euthyphro*. Standard ed. Geneva: Henri Estienne [Stephanus].

Prewitt, Kenneth. 2005. "Racial Classification in America: Where Do We Go from Here?" *Daedalus* 134, no. 1: 5–17.

Root, Michael. 2000. "How We Divide the World." *Philosophy of Social Science* 67(Suppl): 628–639.

Rosen, Gideon. 1994. "Objectivity and Modern Idealism: What Is the Questions?" In *Philosophy in Mind*, edited by John O'Leary-Hawthorne and Michaelis Michael, 277–319. Dortrecth: Kluwer Academic Publishers.

Rorty, Amélie, and David Wong. 1993. "Aspects of Identity and Agency." In *Identity, Character, and Morality: Essays in Moral Psychology*, edited by Owen Flanagan and Amélie Rorty, 19–36. Cambridge, MA: Bradford Book / MIT Press.

Roughgarden, Joan. 2004. *Evolution's Rainbow: Diversity, Gender, and Sexuality in Nature and People*. Berkeley: University of California Press.

Saul, Jennifer Mather. 2012. "Politically Significant Terms and the Philosophy of Language: Methodological Issues." In *Out from the Shadows: Analytical Feminist Contributions to Traditional Philosophy*, edited by Sharon L. Crasnow and Anita M. Superson, 196–216. Oxford: Oxford University Press.

Searle, John. 1969. *Speech Acts: An Essay in the Philosophy of Language*. Cambridge: Cambridge University Press.

———. 1979. *Expression and Meaning: Studies in the Theory of Speech Acts*. Cambridge: Cambridge University Press.

———. 1983. *Intentionality: An Essay in the Philosophy of Mind*. Cambridge: Cambridge University Press.

———. 1997. *The Construction of Social Reality*. New York: Free Press.

———. 2010. *Making the Social World: The Structure of Human Civilization*. New York: Oxford University Press.

Silvers, Anita, and Leslie Francis. 2017. "An Americans with Disabilities Act for Everyone, and for the Ages as Well." *The Cardozo Law Review* 39 no. 2: 669–697.

Sink, Larry. 1997. "Race and Ethnicity Classification Consistency between the Census Bureau and the National Center for Health Statistics." Population Division Working Paper No. 17, U.S. Census Bureau, February. https://www.census.gov/population/www/documentation/twps0017/.

Smith, Michael. 1989. "Dispositional Theories of Value." *Proceedings of the Aristotelian Society Supplement* 63: 89–111.

Snipp, M. C. 2003. "Racial Measurement in the American Census: Past Practices and Implications for the Future." *Annual Review of Sociology* 29: 563–588.

Solnit, Rebecca. 2010. *Infinite City: A San Francisco Atlas*. Berkeley: University of California Press.

Spencer, Quayshawn. 2012. "What 'Biological Racial Realism' Should Mean." *Philosophical Studies* 159, no. 2: 181–204.

Stalnaker, Robert. 1999. *Context and Content: Essays on Intentionality in Speech and Thought.* Oxford: Oxford University Press.

Stoljar, Natalie. 1995. "Essence, Identity, and the Concept of Woman." *Philosophical Topics* 23, no. 2: 261–293.

———. 2011. "Different Women. Gender and the Realism-Nominalism Debate." In *Feminist Metaphysics*, edited by Charlotte Witt, 27–46. Dortrecht: Springer.

Sundstrom, Ronald. 2002. "Racial Nominalism." *Journal of Social Philosophy* 33, no. 2: 193–210.

UNESCO. 1967. *Four Statements on the Race Question.* Paris: UNESCO.

Wendell, Susan. 1990. *The Rejected Body.* New York: Routledge.

Wiggins, David. 1976. "Truth, Invention, and the Meaning of Life." *Proceedings of the British Academy* 62: 331–378.

Witt, Charlotte. 2011. *The Metaphysics of Gender.* Oxford: Oxford University Press.

Wright, Crispin. 1992. *Truth and Objectivity.* Cambridge, MA: Harvard University Press.

Young, Iris Marion. 1989. "Polity and Group Difference: A Critique of the Idea of Universal Citizenship." *Ethics* 99: 250–274.

Zack, Naomi. 1993. *Race and Mixed Race.* Philadelphia: Temple University Press.

INDEX

Page numbers followed by n indicate notes.

Longino, Helen, 55n3
looping effect, 51, 122
Ludwig, Kirk, 21n14
Lugones, María, 5–6, 117

Mallon, Ron, 34–35, 41n10, 52–53
marriage equality movement, 89
materialist feminism, 82
McGowan, Mary Kate, 15, 19
metaphysics, 55n3
Michigan Womyn's Festival, 90
Mills, Charles, 103, 106
Mitford, Nancy, 14n9, 50
Mixed/Multiple ethnic groups (racial category), 105
Moi, Toril, 54n2
Muslims, 107–8

Native Americans. *See* American Indian or Alaska Native (racial category)
Native Hawaiian or Other Pacific Islander (racial category), 96
nature, 56
Nazism, 109
nominalism, 107
noninevitability, 34–35
norms
  behavior, 119–20
  gender, 120n2
  social, 86
North Carolina, 77–79
noumenal realm, 65–66

objectification, 63–64, 121
objective identity, 82, 122
objective ramification, 115
objective social identity, 122
oppression, 127–28
Other ethnic group (racial category), 105
others, 73n5

passing, 117, 123–24
perception, 27–28
permissibility facts, 19
phenomenal realm, 65–66
physical disability, 112
piety, 7

population, 85
properties. *See also* social properties
  communal, 24–25
public identity, 82

queerness, 1n1

race
  as communal construct, 102–4
  as institutional construct, 93–102
  in other contexts, 104–5
  self-identification of, 102
  as social construct, 42–44, 106
  views on, 106–7
racial categories
  communal, 102–4
  conferral of, 90, 106–7, 107n17
  institutional, 93–102
radical linguistic constructivism, 59–60
ramification, 115
Rayo, Agustín, 73n5
realism, 35n2
reality, social, 16–17
refugees, 45–46
regulative rules, 119
regulatory ideals, 61–65
religious categories, 90, 107–10
representation, 52
response dependence, 12–13, 12n7, 24–31, 26n21, 91–92
Roman Catholic Church, 88–89
Rorty, Amélie, 115
rules, 119

Saint-Croix, Cat, 125n3
salience. *See* social significance
Saul, Jennifer, 87n16
Searle, John, 9, 13, 16–17, 26–28
Second Sex (Beauvoir), 54–55
self-conception, 115–17
self-conferral, 24, 25n20
self-identification, 102
self-presentation, 89
semantic contextualism, 87
sex, 54–69
  definition of, 42
  materiality of, 60, 63

CPSIA information can be obtained
at www.ICGtesting.com
Printed in the USA
BVHW030315300819

557080BV00002B/7/P

9 780190 256807